THE LEISURE ARCHITECTURE OF

Wayne McAllister

THE LEISURE ARCHITECTURE OF
Wayne McAllister

CHRIS NICHOLS

Gibbs Smith, Publisher
TO ENRICH AND INSPIRE HUMANKIND

Salt Lake City | Charleston | Santa Fe | Santa Barbara

First Edition
11 10 09 08 07   5 4 3 2 1

Text © 2007 Chris Nichols
Photographs © 2007 as noted on page 157

Published by
Gibbs Smith, Publisher
P.O. Box 667
Layton, Utah 84041

Orders: 1.800.835.4993
www.gibbs-smith.com

Designed by Kurt Wahlner
Printed and bound in Hong Kong

Library of Congress Cataloging-in-Publication Data
Nichols, Chris.
    The leisure architecture of Wayne McAllister / Chris Nichols. — 1st ed.
        p. cm.
    Includes index.
    ISBN-13: 978-1-58685-699-1
1. McAllister, Wayne, 1907-2000—Themes, motives.
2. Restaurants—United States—History—20th century.
3. Hotels—United States—History—20th century. I. Title.

NA737.M218N53 2007
720.92—dc22
                                                    2006021018

Contents

If YOU ARE IN ANY WAY DISPLEASED WITH YOUR FOOD, YOUR WAITRESS WILL CHEERFULLY EXCHANGE IT FOR ANY OTHER ITEM.

Preface

Bob's Big Boy, Burbank.
McAllister's classic 1949
drive-in is a state landmark.

Plans were announced in early 1991 for a new office building to rise in Burbank, California. It would be another in a row of anonymous black slabs that lined Riverside Drive from the Warner Brothers Studios to NBC. The "Media District" was growing and would soon supplant a small drive-in restaurant Wayne McAllister had designed in 1949.

For the past four decades, the towering thirty-five-foot neon sign at this Bob's Big Boy had served as a beacon for the families, aerospace workers and studio employees of Burbank to congregate at this community gathering spot. Coffee shops are democratic places—places where everyone orders off the same menu; where no seat (or customer) is better than another; where friends had met and continued to meet for generations.

I joined the Los Angeles Conservancy Modern Committee four years after it was formed in 1984. The founders organized after the demolition of two other landmark coffee shops and were not about to see Bob's go without a fight. I supported the effort because my parents were coffee shop junkies. Mom and Dad dated at The Huddle and eventually dragged me along to every Sambo's, Denny's and Bob's in Southern California. I remember the looks my father would get from disgruntled waitresses after the sixteenth refill of that never-ending cup of coffee.

My father gave me a copy of Alan Hess' book *Googie: Fifties Coffee Shop Architecture* and it changed my life. I saw that there was an order and a genus to this strange species—the California coffee shop—that had become so familiar. The coffee shops had a lineage and an evolution and were created by these genius architects nobody had ever heard of. They had once been fantastic creations with designs inspired by a World's Fair or science fiction movie. Hess showed us that by creating a new architecture based on serving the automobile and an understanding of the radically changing cityscape of booming Los Angeles, architects like Armet & Davis, Martin Stern and Wayne McAllister were the unsung heroes of the commercial strip.

The Modern Committee formed a task force to determine whether Bob's Big Boy was eligible for the California Register of Historical Places. In the course of our research we discovered Wayne McAllister was still at work in a tiny office nearby.

In January 1992 he agreed to participate in an oral history project that became the basis of a successful landmark nomination. After the state's decision to make Bob's Big Boy a historical landmark, owner Phillip MacDonald changed his plans to destroy the shop and embarked on an ambitious restoration: new neon, rehabbed interiors, a vintage-themed marketing campaign, and the hiring of the first new carhops in decades. The restaurant subsequently became the highest-grossing Big Boy restaurant in the country.

Five years after the success with Bob's Big Boy, we spotted Wayne at breakfast in a Pasadena coffee shop. His wife, Corinne, was by his side, and he was open and easy with conversations about people and places that had long passed. Even as he was approaching ninety, he spoke

McAllister, exhibit designer Michael Palumbo and author look over blueprints displayed at a 1998 Pacific Design Center tribute. The Los Angeles Conservancy feted McAllister on his ninety-first birthday with a retrospective lecture and exhibit.

with the rapid rat-a-tat-tat dialogue and hepcat slang of two or three generations before. He recalled in great detail the color schemes and decorative motifs of rooms long ago plowed under and replaced. We spent more and more time together chatting about all the places he and Corinne had created so long ago. I was surprised when he happily accepted an invitation to join me at a screening of early Las Vegas footage at the American Cinematheque. As we watched the jumpy scratched footage of the tiny desert town, Wayne delivered a running dialogue of what flashed across the screen. The audience strained to hear his stunning first-person account of something none of them would ever see.

On November 5, 1998, McAllister received a standing ovation from a capacity house at the Pacific Design Center in West Hollywood. The Conservancy had honored him with a tribute lecture and exhibition that ran for three weeks. The Nevada State Legislature dedicated that day in his honor.

I am lucky and so grateful for the time I was able to spend with Wayne. I miss his quick smile and boisterous laugh.

Acknowledgments

Special thanks to Charlene Gould for being there since the beginning and whose help in writing this book was invaluable.

I would also like to thank the following for their support and assistance: Georgia Allen; Bert Bedeau, Society for Commercial Archeology; Baron Bernard; David Beltran; Adriene Biondo; Kent Bulza; California State Library; Marshall LaPlante; Maria Castillo; Veronica Chavez; Carolyn Cole, Los Angeles Public Library; Volker Corell; Constance Devereaux, Allied Arts Council of Southern Nevada; Dharma Realm Buddhist Association; John English; Helene Federici; Steve Fischer; Richard Frank and Gayle Chick, Lawry's Restaurants, Inc.; Peter and Alice Gowland; Chris Green; Joan Harrison; Jim Heimann; J. Willard Marriott Collection, University of Utah Library; Bruce Herman; J. A. Nichols; Kam Kaminske, Smoke House Restaurant; Kathleen Kelley-Markham; Wally Larson; Alan Leib; Ed Leibowitz; Art Linkletter; Los Angeles Conservancy; Eric Lynxwiler; Nathan Marsak; Russ Mason, Clear Channel Outdoor; Ron May, Legacy 106; Don McAllister and the McAllister family; Dr. Peter Michel, University of Nevada at Las Vegas; Millenium Biltmore Hotel; Peter Moruzzi; Ted Otis; Michael Palumbo; Cheryl and James Pease; Pete Pederson, Gladding McBean Tile Company; Charles Phoenix; Laurene Harding Rivas; San Diego Historical Society; Tiffney Sanford; Janet Barrett Saunders; Gretchen Spence; Mary-Margaret Stratton; Mark Swope; Dace Taube, University of Southern California; Michael Valent; Sara Velas; Marge Walker; Marc Wanamaker, Bison Archives; Eric Warren, Eagle Rock Historical Society; Delmar Watson; Andre Williams; Willie Wilkerson; Lynn Zook; ZZalgern0n.

This book could not exist without the pioneering research and writing of Alan Hess.

Introduction

The architectural legacy of twentieth-century America is not best explained through individual monuments but by the patterns and forms of its places. The spaces that are created and the way people use space dictate a lifestyle. The casual attitude of indoor/ outdoor living generated easy breezy designs. The suburban metropolis of postwar Los Angeles, for example, is better understood through the coffee shops and tract houses than through grand civic buildings or cathedrals. America is a place of free enterprise and visionary ideals, not a place where things are dictated from above.

The forms and spaces designed by architects like Wayne McAllister created much of the character of Southern California. His Fred and Ginger nightclubs and glinting steel and blazing neon

of his circular drive-ins brought Busby Berkeley's Hollywood to life. His Sands Hotel in Las Vegas became the home of the Rat Pack; the mythology of Frank Sinatra, Dean Martin and Sammy Davis Jr. owes a great deal to the swank glamour of the Copa Room at McAllister's finest Nevada hotel.

Wayne McAllister was an iconoclast, a designer with no formal architectural training who would change the fabric of cities, a quiet conservative who created some of the most outlandish and sometimes garish spaces in North America. In 2000 the *New York Times* said that he "elevated commercial structures like the drive-in restaurant and the theme resort to art forms." However, he never appreciated the importance of his own legacy. "A pebble in the lake" is how he once described his work to a reporter, "a spit in the ocean."

"I don't think we had philosophies! People that have philoso-phies are like Neutra and this guy Frank Gehry. Those guys are philosophers and they live in a different world, let's just say that." —Wayne McAllister, 1998

Inside a suite at the Sands Hotel.

Because of this lack of ego, Wayne's work was flexible; he was able to learn and reinvent himself.

Much has been made of the recent growth of Las Vegas. Today the most exclusive boutiques, the finest wines, even the best palm trees have been diverted from Los Angeles to Las Vegas. But the blueprint for the Las Vegas strip was laid by Wayne McAllister in the 1930s with his first plans for El Rancho Vegas. This resort living is defined by the monumental roadside sign at the edge of the highway and the rambling, relaxing scale of everything—generous lawns of green grass flanked by flowers and landscaping and easy parking right outside your door. The beginning of McAllister's hotel work had much in common with the genteel opulence of space found in resort towns like Palm Springs.

It is the sunny and wide-open spaces that most often define his work. His projects always have a leisurely freedom of space, with rolling lawns and open patios. They are often spread out on vast acreage. The hotels with their winding paths or the miles and miles of neon beckoning to the automobile; everything is oriented to the lush landscaping. This openness is a design that would never have worked in his fathers' Pennsylvania.

Wayne was a straight shooter. He was honest but funny in a disarming way. He instantly saw the strengths in people and was endearing and very easy to get along with. He once described a par-ticularly shady business associate as "ugly-looking and he talked like he had mush in his mouth, but he was smart." He could see assets in a difficult person or place and know how to bring them out.

He worked with gangsters, alcoholics, womanizers and corrupt politicians, but he never seemed to be affected by his surroundings. He worked with people without judgment and stayed trustworthy.

He was brilliant in his approach. He knew what the client and the customers wanted. The resort hotels, nightclubs and restaurants he designed were extraordinarily popular and populistic. He was self-trained and didn't have his natural instincts "learned out of him." He would spend months researching a new venture before embarking on it. He became an expert brewmaster, a vendor of children's cartoons and an ostrich farmer in addition to being a master architect. His instincts were right on and his projects often became the most successful of their kind. "Think of how many people have lived in, or even visited, a Frank Lloyd Wright and then compare it to the number who have visited his [Wayne McAllister's] Las Vegas hotels," says architectural historian Alan Hess. "Millions of more people have been influenced and affected by their quality."

ABOVE:
Bar at the Hollywood Plaza Hotel.

RIGHT:
Proof sheet capturing details of the Las Vegas Sands in 1953.

THE WORLD RENOWNED
Biltmore Bowl

BILTMORE HOTEL
LOS ANGELES, CALIFORNIA

the Monocoupe

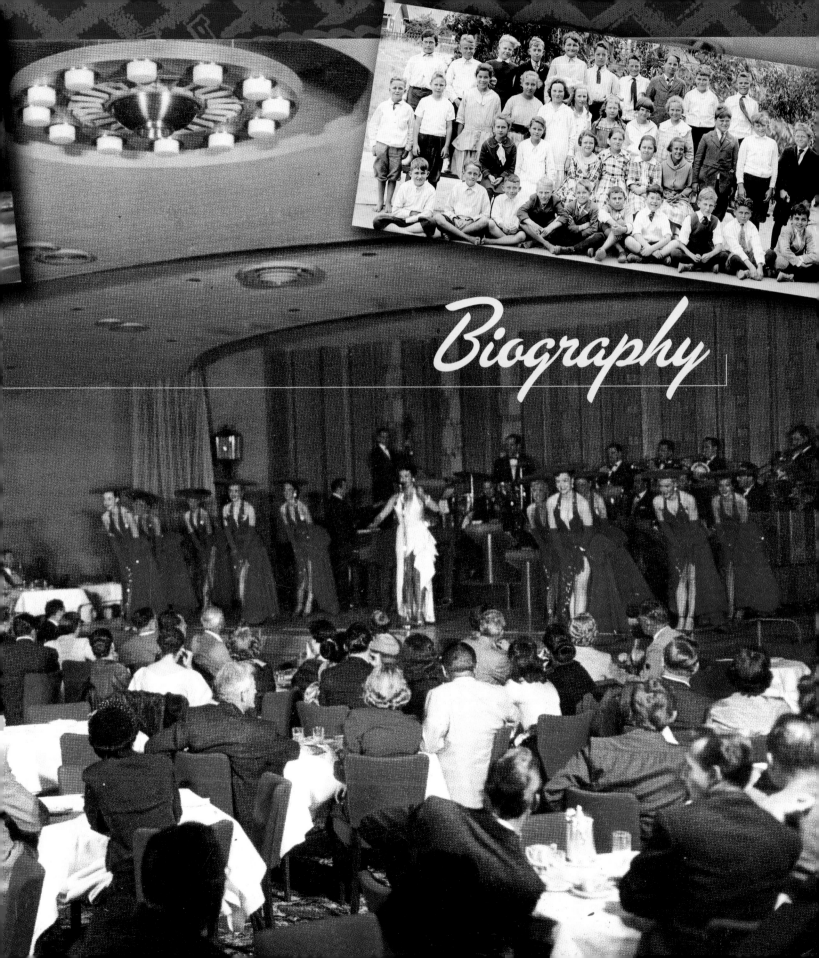

Biography

Downtown Las Vegas, c. 1960.

TOP, LEFT:
The proposal for the
very first resort in
Las Vegas.

ABOVE:
Casino floor at the
Fremont Hotel in Las
Vegas, 1956.

HOTEL PROJECT
Las Vegas, Nevada

Biography

Who "invented" Las Vegas? Why is it there? Why are there 130,000 luxury hotel rooms completely surrounded by hostile wasteland in the middle of the Nevada desert? Contrary to popular belief, gangster Benjamin "Bugsy" Siegel didn't become overheated in the desert and have a vision of a glamorous hotel on the very spot his car broke down. That hotel, the Flamingo, was begun by Billy Wilkerson of *The Hollywood Reporter* and opened in December 1946. The very first resort on what would become the Las Vegas strip was El Rancho Vegas. It was proposed nearly a decade earlier by a trust fund "remittance son" named Jack Barkley and a young architect named Wayne McAllister. A curling and yellowing hand-typed brochure lays

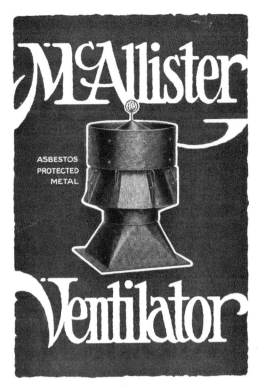

McAllister's father, Albert, was also a clever innovator. Here is a pamphlet for a device he invented to keep sewer gas moving and to prevent exploding commodes.

it all out. "HOTEL PROJECT: LAS VEGAS NEVADA" is the sixteen-page Rosetta stone that helps connect the dots and explain the origins of the strip and of the little-known architect who created it.

EARLY DAYS

He was a reserved man who was once a stunt pilot and a maker of bathtub gin. A native Californian, Wayne was born in San Diego on November 17, 1907, to Albert and Mary McAllister.

Albert was an upstart metalworker whose family followed his craft to the East Coast and back again. He was a divergent thinker—for a century one of his inventions, the McAllister Ventilator, has kept sewage gases moving and prevented exploding lavatories. After a work-related accident claimed Albert in 1919, Mary, Wayne and younger brother Lloyd left Pittsburgh for familiar Southern California.

Growing up in San Diego in the teens must have afforded McAllister an opportunity to visit the lavish Spanish Colonial Revival buildings erected in Balboa Park for the Panama-Pacific Exposition in 1915. Fifteen years later he would propose a theater project for the same park.

LEFT:
Wayne's parents, Albert and Mary McAllister.

ABOVE, LEFT:
Wayne and his mother, Mary, in San Diego, circa 1912. At the height of his architectural practice, McAllister hired his mother as a secretary.

ABOVE, RIGHT:
Detail of elementary school class photo.

During McAllister's last year at San Diego Union High School, it was suggested to the handsome, six-foot-tall lad by a guidance counselor that he should consider a career in "acting or architecture," he recalled, "and I chose the latter." He was always one to take an opportunity when it arose. "Get the job," his first boss told him, "and then figure out how you can do it." He was in the workforce before he completed high school. "I had a photographic memory, and I listened, and I never had to do homework because all I had to do was recall what the teacher had said," he remembered. "So I skidded by pretty well." In what would have been his last semester in high school, Wayne took a full-time job drafting bungalow plans for the Ideal Building Company of San Diego.

In 1925 the lanky ambitious teenager looked across a room of night school drafting students and spotted Corinne Fuller, who happened to be the only female in the class. Corinne was a pretty brunette, a sorority girl who was working as a seamstress. Her employer noticed her artistic talents and suggested that she enroll in a drafting class. With the exception of Julia Morgan, there had never been a licensed female architect in California, yet Corinne was working toward that goal.

An ink drawing, likely by Corinne, with the McAllisters' unbuilt proposal for a theater in Balboa Park, San Diego. The park was originally created in 1915 for the Panama-Pacific Exposition.

The pair enjoyed trips to Mission Beach and dated for about a year while both held full-time jobs in competing architectural offices in downtown San Diego. Corinne worked in the office of well-established architect William Wheeler, and Wayne took a job with the somewhat less prestigious P. Brainerd Hale and his San Diego Architectural Service Bureau (SDASB).

SDASB DAYS

"There was so much competition between lumber companies at that time," remembered McAllister, "that if you bought their lumber, they would give you a plan free." The service bureau performed work for lumber companies but also sold plans through ads in the *San Diego Union-Tribune*. Complete plans were offered at $10 each. McAllister said, "I would draw a plan a day . . . there are houses all over San Diego using my one-day plans."

Some of the success of the SDASB surely must have come from its unwritten policy of allowing city officials, especially a friendly city building inspector, Oscar Kneck, who shepherded plans through the system, access to a private room at their offices. The inspector

Baron Long and his wife at the Biltmore Hotel in Los Angeles. Long, a colorful figure in 1920s Hollywood, became a mentor and friend to McAllister after he hired the young architect to design the Hotel Agua Caliente.

taught Wayne how to meet code and the office offered Kneck a place to bring dates. He and the owner, P. Brainerd Hale, ". . . were fellow womanizers. . . . He had eleven kids and a wooden leg." Hale and McAllister soon became confidantes, and one afternoon in the fall of 1925, Hale took McAllister aside and offered to make him a partner in the business. Wayne eagerly accepted the promotion and helped to lay out a continuation plan, "just in case." The following day, Hale and his new "stripteaser from the local burlesque house" headed over the border into their new life in Mexico, and Wayne McAllister suddenly became the sole proprietor of SDASB.

McAllister was running the SDASB when Mrs. Jack T. Millan came to get plans drawn for a house for the American Building Company, a company she owned with her brother-in-law and her husband, who was city treasurer of San Diego. The company offered building plans, construction and financing for residential and small commercial buildings. One of these, the Beatty House, is landmark #674 of the city of San Diego.

According to Wayne, Jack T. Millan "was a big man, a cripple. He was stricken with polio after he first came into office. . . . He had to have crutches, but with his affliction the city affectionately took him over and kept electing him. He was the behind-the-scenes politician for San Diego. He was with a group who handpicked the mayor and the city council."

Millan was a sought-after ally for those who wanted to do business in San Diego, a direct link to city hall for anyone seeking influence. When Millan incorporated the American Building Company in December 1926, one of his first stockholders was the "large, jovial and personable" Baron Long, who saw value in having the insider on his team. Long became McAllister's mentor and friend for decades.

AGUA CALIENTE DAYS

Corinne McAllister drew much of the intricate detail work for the Hotel Agua Caliente by hand. This small piece of vellum showing a detail of a griffin is all that she retained from her drawings of the hotel.

McAllister always had a knack for observing the changing landscape and moving with it. He was able to act fast and take advantage of opportunities that others may not have noticed. Through Baron Long, he was able to spin his unique ideas into a winning proposal for a $10 million resort just over the Mexican border called Agua Caliente before he turned twenty.

In the evenings, Corinne and Wayne collaborated on the design. He laid out rooms and equipment and she created the intricate design details that completed the plan. The two dated and worked on side projects together for two years when they drove 100 miles north to Santa Ana and were quietly married in 1926.

THIS PAGE AND OPPOSITE:
Tourist snapshots of the Hotel Agua Caliente, 1935.

When William Wheeler discovered that a competing architect had not only won the huge Agua Caliente project but had also married one of his top designers, Corinne was terminated. She immediately joined Wayne in finishing the plans for the hotel. With Wheeler serving as president of the state architectural board, he vowed that "as long as I have anything to do with the board of architectural examiners in California, you will never get a license."

Wayne McAllister and . . .

McAllister managed without a license for decades, often scratching out the word *architect* on building permits and substituting the word *designer* or adding the cryptic "U.C." after his signature—personal shorthand for "Uncertified."

They were also working on smaller projects in San Diego while designing Agua Caliente, including a competition for a new theater in Balboa Park.

BALBOA BEER DAYS

By 1933, when prohibition, the very foundation of Agua Caliente's success, was ending as the Eighteenth Amendment was near repeal, Baron Long decided to position himself to take full advantage of fifteen years of bottled-up demand for alcohol in America. He again called on his clever young friend McAllister . . . McAllister's only previous experience in the liquor business was limited to what he created in his own home. McAllister recalled that . . .

BALBOA BREWING CO. — LOS ANGELES, CALIF.

McAllister became vice president of Balboa Brewing Company in 1933. The beer was such a success that McAllister moved to Los Angeles in 1934 to supervise the construction of a larger plant in his new hometown.

Every Friday night, we would bust out a gallon of alcohol, which we would get through the dentists or the doctors—they were the bootleggers. They had permits to buy alcohol, which came in a gallon tin can. We would pay five dollars for a can of alcohol and with that we could make two and a half gallons of forty-proof gin. You mix the two together, water and alcohol, and with an eyedropper you drop so many drops of juniper oil in it, that was the flavoring, and then you would age it. You'd wait about five minutes before you drank it. And then we, of course, had to brown bag it if we went out anyplace where we were going to a restaurant or dance floor. . . . We would go out Friday night and Saturday night, and four or six of us maybe would go together, and we would kill that gallon over the weekend. And sometimes it would kill us . . . oh boy, talk about everything tasting and looking black on Sunday morning.

McAllister learned every step of the process and became an expert brewer. Long and his investors founded the Ritz Brewing Company at the end of 1933. When someone spooked them with the warning "People will say Ritz is the shits," Long and McAllister changed the beer's name to Balboa, recruiting the Spanish explorer as their mascot. Balboa was founded in a brick warehouse on Imperial Avenue in San Diego and McAllister was named vice president. The following year they expanded north to Los Angeles.

There was so much demand by the following year that the entire operation and its young vice president moved to Los Angeles, where McAllister manned three shifts twenty-four hours a day, seven days a week, and created 108,000 barrels of beer a year. Balboa thrived as the tap beer of choice in Southern California, but its short run came to an end after just a few years.

McAllister would never again sell beer, but he did create some of the most memorable bars and nightclubs in Southern California. He would design the rooms stars played and dined in, and the room in which the Academy Awards were held. He would also

TOP:
Mike Lyman's Grill in downtown Los Angeles.

———

ABOVE:
The iconic roadside sign at the Las Vegas Sands.

———

RIGHT:
After designing so many restaurants, McAllister tried to operate one of his own: the failed Golden Lantern restaurant in Denver, Colorado.

design iconic drive-in restaurants with signs larger than the buildings and bring outdoor living to legendary hotels. He took some of the most challenging architecture in America to the streets, where it enhanced the lives of millions of people. In 1941 he and hotelier Thomas Hull invented the form and flavor of the Las Vegas strip. They set the pattern, style and approach with their El Rancho Vegas Resort Hotel.

LAS VEGAS DAYS

After the start of World War II, building contracts became scarcer. Soon, almost all essential building materials would be commandeered for the war effort. McAllister was thirty-four years old and nearly out of work. Ever the entrepreneur, he shuttered the architectural practice and opened a machine shop, the McAllister Airparts Company, on Sunset Boulevard in Hollywood. His next move was completely unexpected: Wayne and Corinne decided to leave the home they had recently built for themselves, a traditional number with streamline Moderne details, nestled in the hills of Los Feliz. They packed up their two young sons and joined another couple in a move to Denver, Colorado, where, with no experience running a restaurant, they opened the Golden Lantern. The partnership eventually dissolved and so did the McAllisters' marriage. They divorced in 1942.

After the war, the McAllisters returned to Los Angeles, where they remarried and relaunched the architectural practice. Wayne's nightclub designs for Los Angeles underworld figures drew him back to Las Vegas, designing hotels for Benjamin "Bugsy" Siegel and Meyer Lansky. He created the first high-rise hotel in downtown Las Vegas, the Fremont, in 1956.

TOP:
McAllister remodeled the El Cortez in Las Vegas for Benjamin "Bugsy" Siegel.

———

CENTER AND BOTTOM:
Architectural renderings of McAllister's Las Vegas hotels.

J. Willard Marriott's chain of restaurants on eastern highways and turn-pikes began in 1927 as an A&W Root Beer operation. Marriott enjoyed terrific success with drive-in restaurants and pioneering food service operations, and by the 1950s, he wanted to expand into hotel lodging.

Marriott had been touring California every summer, scouting out new restaurant ideas, when he was introduced to McAllister, and knowing Wayne's business reputation, Marriott pursued him for years. In 1956, after his success in luring McAllister to Washington, Marriott made him vice president in charge of architecture for Marriott's Hot Shoppes. McAllister supervised the very first hotels developed by Marriott. Their first venture was the 365-room Twin Bridges Motor Hotel in Arlington, Virginia, which opened in 1957.

J. Willard Marriott founded the chain of Hot Shoppes restaurants on Eastern highways and turnpikes. It began in 1927 as an A&W Root Beer operation. Marriott enjoyed terrific success with drive-in restaurants and pioneering food service operations.

———————

RIGHT:
Details of J. Willard Marriott's Hot Shoppes, supervised by McAllister after he left his own practice to work for the budding hotel magnate. These were his last restaurants before he supervised the construction of the first Marriott Hotel in Arlington, Virginia.

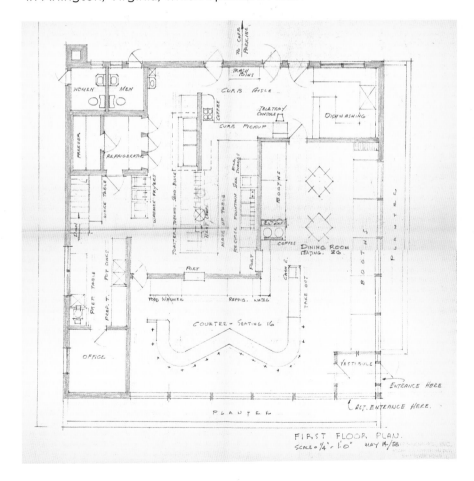

McAllister stopped designing full time at the age of forty-nine. He had signed a five-year contract with Marriott, and when it was up in 1961, he decided not to renew and planned a return to Southern California. He stopped in Newport Beach and then Pasadena. For the next four decades McAllister began a variety of entrepreneurial endeavors, reinventing himself again and again. He pursued commercial ostrich farming, cartoon kiosks and eventually represented one of the world's first coin-operated copy machines. In 1999 he returned to architecture with a series of tract houses in Yucaipa, California.

His last office was in a rambling old warehouse in a manufacturing district in Alhambra, California. He worked there until his death in 2000. While traveling from his office to a routine medical appointment, Wayne McAllister fell and hit his head on the sidewalk. He spent two weeks in a coma and died on March 22, 2000, in Arcadia, California. He was survived by Corinne, his sons, Don and David, and his daughter, Paulette. Corinne moved near David in Phoenix, where she died on November 28, 2001.

Three decades of groundbreaking commissions, from the return of Hollywood nightlife after Prohibition to futuristic drive-ins to the very first resort hotel in Las Vegas, all traced their origins back to that first hotel in the desert outside Tijuana: Agua Caliente.

Wayne and Corinne were married for almost seventy-five years. They enjoyed playing with their family and grandkids by the pool of their Pasadena home.

OPPOSITE:
Portrait of Wayne McAllister, c. 1930.

Viva!

CAREFREE

Caliente

AMERICA'S
DEAUVILLE
completely equipped
for
Mental Relaxation
Physical Development
and Entertainment

AGUA CALIENTE
INVITES YOU

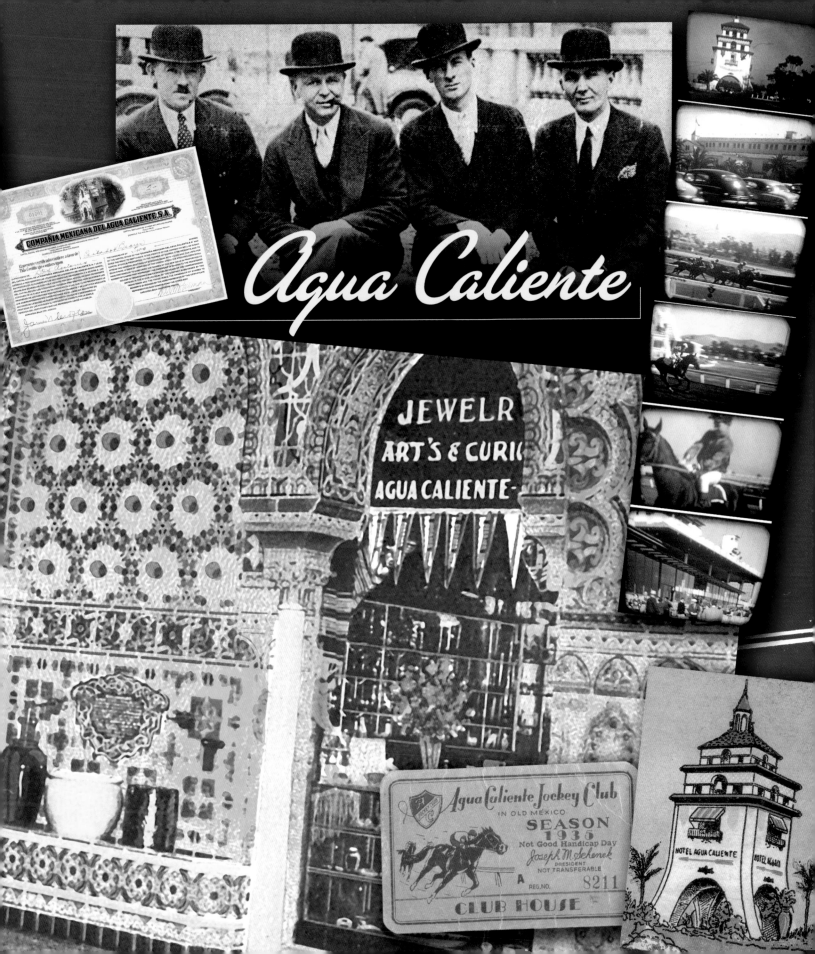

Agua Caliente

Agua Caliente

Agua Caliente was one of the most opulent resorts ever to grace the Americas, but more significantly, it was the inspiration for Las Vegas, created during a time when horse racing, gambling and drinking were all illegal. In the west, wealthy hedonistic Americans migrated south into Mexico to indulge in sin and luxury. America's social constraints were the catalysts for such a resort, but only one man could envision every detail and, most importantly, bring his vision to fruition: Wayne McAllister.

Backed by a cast of colorful characters, Wayne was a teenage high school dropout without a license to practice architecture. Agua Caliente was the opportunity Wayne needed to set in motion his legacy of fantastic escapist resorts.

From Agua Caliente's initial planning, function and clientele to its architecture and advertising campaign, its draw and lure foretold an inevitable American counterpart, but none would approach it until the rise of Las Vegas decades later. Though Vegas' legacy outshines that of Caliente, it falls short when compared to Agua Caliente's luxurious amenities, its epic scale and architectural embellishments; for Caliente was unprecedented and never duplicated.

Cheap trinkets, vice and squalor abound in present-day Tijuana, with its ramshackle storefronts and rutted streets. In the 1920s Avenida Revolucion was described by *Vogue* as ". . . dirty streets swarming with boisterous crowds and lined with slot machines, bottles of whisky and perfume, and red and green Mexican rugs . . . ," but the surrounding land was much more pastoral.

The entire project was conceived by Baron Long, James Crofton and Wirt Bowman. The trio was empowered by Governor General Abelardo Rodriguez of Mexico. During this same period McAllister was still drawing plans for simple homes for Millan's American Building Company in San Diego. When the American

THE FOREIGN CLUB

The Foreign Club was a gambling center before the rise of Agua Caliente. The simple structures seemed quite austere when compared to the glories of the new gambling resort.

ABOVE:
An idealized postcard view showing the main entrance to Hotel Agua Caliente, Tijuana, Mexico. McAllister and Baron Long imagined a resort hotel that greeted the weary traveler with the romance of an ancient mission.

RIGHT:
Agua Caliente was 655 acres and included its own airport.

Building Company became a corporation, the first major stockholder was Baron Long. Bowman, Crofton and Rodriguez soon joined him as partners.

Perhaps the most colorful character of all was a man McAllister considered his most important mentor, Baron Long. Born in Indiana in August 1883, Long came to Los Angeles in 1908 as a promoter and assistant to famed boxer Jim Jeffries at the Vernon Arena, which was just outside Los Angeles. He established a name for himself in the teens as the leading promoter of organized boxing in Los Angeles. In 1912 he took over the lease of the nearby Vernon Country Club. Operating outside the Los Angeles city limits in the independent city of Vernon (founded in 1905 as the first exclusively industrial city in the southwestern United States), Long was able to skirt prohibition laws and operate the "world's longest bar." His Vernon Country Club, quite a distance from Hollywood, was an immediate draw for the burgeoning film colony there. It attracted the likes of Mary Pickford, Fatty Arbuckle and Gloria Swanson to its remote location. One of Rudolph Valentino's first professional jobs was as a tango instructor at the club.

Since the passing of the Eighteenth Amendment banning alcohol, Long, a former patent medicine salesman, was soon offering his popular blend of legal drinking, nightclub entertainment and gambling at the Watts Tavern and the Ship Café in Venice. He expanded into the hotel business with his purchase of the U. S. Grant Hotel, a pillar of downtown San Diego. With future projects in mind, Long developed an interest in city politics, where he met Jack T. Millan and invested in the American Building Company.

Long realized that the ban on drinking, gambling and horse racing extended only a few miles past San Diego and that beyond the American border an "anything goes" mentality prevailed. In 1926 Long, Bowman, Crofton and Rodriguez secured a concession to build a new spa at the Agua Caliente Hot Springs, located six miles from the United States border in Tijuana. The partners imagined a massive resort, a city of entertainment close

Agua Caliente partner James Crofton and Wayne McAllister disembark from an epic rail expedition of racetracks around the United States in 1929 before building a grand track at their gambling resort.

enough to draw the same moneyed Hollywood crowd as the Vernon Country Club that Long had established, yet operating freely, easily and legally in Mexico.

Abelardo Rodriguez had been a general in the Mexican army. He became governor of Northern Baja California in 1921 and was named military commander in 1923. President Plutarco Elias Calles of Mexico granted a concession to Rodriguez for the rights to build a spa using the natural hot-water springs. At the height of Agua Caliente's success, Rodriguez became president of Mexico, a puppet to Calles.

James Crofton ran the gambling of the Foreign Club, an older gambling hall in Tijuana. He was the perfect person to head up the casino and racetrack at Agua Caliente. Although the original concession was for a water resort, the spa was the second tier of the development.

Wirt Bowman owned and operated the Foreign Club. He worked for the Southern Pacific Railroad before becoming a rancher in Nogales, Mexico. He was also a banker in Nogales, Arizona, across the border from Nogales, Mexico, and was the primary financier for American projects in Mexico.

These investors of the new project, christened Agua Caliente, after the ancient mineral springs that dotted the site, commissioned plans for its construction. Long decided that a project of such magnitude required an architectural competition to determine the best design. Plans were submitted by some of the leading architects in Southern California. One after another, the architects' drawings failed to capture the romance that Long had envisioned.

William Wheeler was the leading establishment architect in San Diego and was the president of the board of architectural examiners for the state of California. Wheeler's plans called for a rather staid and formal Italianate style. He was so sure he would get the job that he took out advertisements for the new project.

The next approach had Baron looking closer to home. Long owned stock in the American Building Company, and with Millan's

The picturesque road leading to the hotel was dotted with ancient sycamore trees.

urging, offered the opportunity for McAllister to give it a try. When Baron Long drove Millan's teenage partner down to the site that would become Agua Caliente, it was a vast acreage of barren scrub dotted by a few ancient sycamore trees. An imaginary story of the resort unfolded from Long, who envisioned a place built ". . . by a group of old Spanish missionaries as they worked their way up the coast," a place they would stay "at the end of the day's ride from the last mission. . . . I talked of a campanile and of the sunset being

Costumed bellmen in silk sashes and gaucho hats were part of the theme at Agua Caliente.

mirrored off gleaming white walls and of an air of peace and quiet, of bells ringing vespers and walks bordered by rich flowers of the tropics, of trees where no trees had stood before."

The young designer, unfettered by tradition or reputation, set out to give the client what he wanted, an ethos he carried throughout his career. According to columnist John G. Thomson of the *San Diego Herald,*

Scarcely daring to hope, Long went to bed that night to dream once more of that which was close to his heart. Not so, young McAllister. Sitting up all night, he drew plans of the great enterprise—for he, where all others had failed, had captured the vision as seen through the eyes of another—had captured it perfectly. The next morning, before Long had awakened, McAllister had finished his rough pencil sketches. With breathless enthusiasm, he carried them to Long's bedside. It did not take much time for Long to see that his quest was over. He had found his man. Together they would plan the miracle that is Agua Caliente.

By 1927 the governor general, the banker, the gambling expert and the maverick hotelier agreed on a plan for Agua Caliente. This was certainly not going to be a replica of the rough-hewn chapels of Junipero Serra, but it was to recollect the distant romance of such places. This place would have a Louis XIV room, a Moorish spa and an art deco dining room inspired directly from the 1925 Exposition Internationale des Arts Décoratifs et Industriels Modernes in Paris. McAllister remembered, "My decorator [Anthony Heinsbergen] went to the expo and brought back . . . the Zigzag Moderne style, which we did in the dining room. That was our first start of Moderne."

The teenage architect's fantasy world so appealed to Long, he turned the job over to the nineteen-year-old designer who suddenly announced that he was now twenty-seven. A project of this magnitude—a hotel, spa and casino on 655 acres of natural Tijuana river valley—would be entirely drawn by Wayne, Corinne and one

draftsman, a high school friend named Eddie Springer. In the center would be a 400-plus-room luxury hotel, several cocktail bars and fine dining in opulent surroundings. There would be Monte Carlo–style gaming rooms: roulette, baccarat and faro. There would be an eighteen-hole championship 180-acre golf course, home to the richest tournament ever held, with spectator porches and floodlights for night play. There was a pitch-and-putt golf course, championship tennis courts, a riding academy, a racetrack that would hold the $140,000 Agua Caliente handicap (the richest in the world at the time), a rail line and even a small airport. The budget would eventually reach $10 million. Based on a percentage of the GDP at the time of its completion, that figure today would be over two billion dollars.

In 1929 *Architectural Digest* published a sixteen-page spread on the hotel and described Agua Caliente this way: "As one approaches the entrada of the main hotel, the ensemble of white, mosaic-tiled buildings shows in its architectural beauty the influence of the Padres. In the vestibula is felt the warmth and hospitable atmosphere of the old world. A huge fireplace invites leisure and comfort. Doors leading into the Avenida de las Palmas lure the visitor through a large courtyard, fragrant with flowers."

The hotel opened Saturday, June 23, 1928, and was an instant success. The complex was built in multiple phases continuously with a seemingly unlimited budget. The expansion of Agua Caliente would become the entire output of the McAllister office for the next several years. The first structure was a 300-foot lamella-roofed parking garage that served as base camp. The hotel opened with fifty-six guest rooms, bungalows and a casino. It was quickly expanded with an additional two-story building with over 300 rooms behind the original. The beautifully detailed bungalows foreshadowed the free and easy cabanas set into landscaping at places like the Los Angeles Ambassador. Only a decade earlier, trailer courts and tourist cabins were alternatives to the traditional multistory hotel.

In 1930 McAllister completed fifty additional bungalows at the east end of the Agua Caliente property. These were set among

ABOVE:
The hotel lobby, decorated by Louis Sherman.

RIGHT:
The supporting members of the lobby ceiling were heavily
carved and connected with steel straps. Enormous Aztec-
inspired candelabra chandeliers adorn the soaring lobby space.

existing mature sycamore trees and looked as if they had always been there. The units have a similar layout but sport varying facades with recurring Spanish themes of stucco, tile and arched windows.

Given carte blanche to create the sumptuous environment Long and the investors dreamed of, McAllister commissioned building materials from leading manufacturers and enlisted the help of interior designer Louis G. Sherman to outfit the guest rooms. Even the modest three-chair barbershop was slathered with dozens of patterns of custom terra-cotta. A 150-foot-tall smokestack from the power plant was tiled and encrusted with ornamental ironwork to become a minaret. Wayne and Corinne began to amass voluminous clipping files with architectural details cribbed from great monuments of the world: fantastic combinations that only existed in their library of reference books; magazine clippings; and plates and drawings provided by manufacturers and suppliers.

The backers were anxious to get the casino running, and when the spa portion of the project lagged, they received pressure to complete the original concession. The bathhouse was perhaps the most lavishly decorated space at the resort, with its incredible mass of art tile. Ed Genter at Gladding McBean was the ceramics designer on the project, and this was the largest installation completed for the legendary tile manufacturer. Every surface of the soaring space was covered in heavily detailed three-dimensional plaster reliefs or tile. Authentic Moorish filigree designs in metal and glass served as skylights in the bathhouse, allowing natural light to stream through. Elaborate lighting effects were employed at the swimming pool, where three colors of neon were hidden behind glass along the coving. The neon could be turned on in any combination to create unique color combinations. The Olympic-sized, aqua-tiled main pool connected to a children's pool by a shallow walkway with a grand fountain at the center. Portions remain to this day.

When the old Jockey Club nearby was decommissioned in 1929, Agua Caliente gained a new racetrack. McAllister became the junior member of an international tour of horse-racing operations.

CLOCKWISE FROM ABOVE:

The spa building was the initial concession for a new resort at the site of the ancient mineral springs at Agua Caliente. Here is the poolside view of the spa building.

———

The entrance to the spa and bathhouse is marked by a terra-cotta figure of Pan playing the flute. This sculpture survived the decades only to be destroyed by vandals.

The spa interiors were part of the largest ceramic tile installation to date by the Gladding McBean Tile Company. Walls, floors and ceilings were lined with elaborately patterned tile, and the room was appointed in a Moorish motif.

———

Gladding McBean artist Ed Genter designed the tiled interior of the spa.

ABOVE:
The Agua Caliente racetrack hosted such equine legends as Phar Lap and Seabiscuit.

BELOW, LEFT:
On race night, 5,600 people packed the grand-stands. Horse racing would continue here into the 1990s. The site currently hosts greyhound races.

BELOW, RIGHT:
Betting windows were "leaded" with silver and nickel geometric patterns.

They visited existing racetracks all over the Americas. McAllister and Crofton were joined by Marshall Cassidy, a starter from New York and Chicago, and John P. Mills, another stockholder. They were even pictured wearing matching bowlers in the *New York Daily Post.* On their trip they saw tracks in Chicago, Montreal, Toronto, New York, Maryland, Miami and Havana—including Arlington Park, Belmont Park, Laurel and Pimlico. They flew from Miami to Cuba on one of the first international over-water flights ever offered on the same Fokker planes made famous by the Red Baron. In Cuba, they drank beer imported from Germany. They got home on June 1, 1929. Despite the stock market crash that October, the track had to open Christmas Day. Grading the track required moving seven million feet of cubic earth. According to Wayne, "It was really seven feet out of level." The horses ran "half going up and half going down." He said that horses that ran a mile would time out right but those that ran the $5/8$ mile would always be slightly off. The five-story grandstands were poured concrete with a massive basement that became the hotel wine cellar. There was lawn for standing room in front of the stands, boxes for the elite and a press box on top of the stands. It was a thoroughbred racetrack with grandstands seating 5,600. Even with the tight building schedule, the stands had many of the same architectural features as the hotel. Red-tile roofs, smooth stucco walls and turned columns flanked a colonnade decorated with a carved marble relief with gargoyles in niches created in Italy. Striped canvas covered spectators in the grandstands. The betting was in a spectacular art deco room with silver and nickel geometric leaded-glass payout windows.

Guests traveled a palm-lined boulevard that ran from the campanile at the highway to the main entrance of the hotel. The ancient pepper trees that inspired Long's vision remained, sheltering a long cloister of adobe arches and the entrance arcade that culminated at a massive Mission Revival entry pavilion. Stationed at the entrance arch were costumed bellmen with gaucho hats and silk sashes, inviting visitors up the stairs past a pair of enormous oil urns and into the soaring lobby space with its exposed truss ceiling.

The campanile was an imposing roadside landmark and became the symbol of the hotel. Its function was mainly as a sign, but its iconic image became a symbol of Tijuana and was featured on hotel stationery, postcards and luggage labels.

The tiled fountain in the courtyard dining area. Terra-cotta gargoyles peer from the center.

The supporting members were heavily carved and connected with steel straps, each beam painted in zigzags and wavy patterns. From these hung enormous Aztec-inspired candelabra chandeliers, and brocade tapestries were hung over doorways on iron rods.

The clay-tiled patio was dominated by a tall terra-cotta fountain adorned with gargoyle heads designed by Gladding McBean. This fountain was placed in a seventeen-sided, star-shaped pool decorated with Moorish tile, resting in a grassy spot in the center of the dining area. A columned esplanade led to the indoor dining room and kitchens. Tables and chairs were intricately carved and highly decorated.

The adjacent pool and spa area was dominated by the 150-foot-tall minaret, which hid the smokestack of the boiler room. The pool area was heavily landscaped in tropical palms and desert yuccas. Canvas director chairs lined the Olympic-sized pool, with a shallow end cordoned off by a glazed terra-cotta nymph fountain for young swimmers. The pool was lined with turquoise and black tile, and from it one could gaze back at the red clay roof, wrought-iron railings and arched windows of the bathhouse. The opposite entrance, facing the hotel, was a two-story space dominated by a brightly colored glazed-tile tower and a second-story breezeway of arches on columns. The cast-stone entrance, punctuated by iron lanterns and intricate window grilles, was reached by stairs and was dominated by a life-sized sculpture of Pan emerging from an enormous shell and playing his pipes.

The main ballroom was the hub of entertainment at Agua Caliente. Entertainers would perform under a red-and-black and silver-leafed vaulted ceiling dizzyingly decorated with art deco zigzags and outrageous colorful patterns. Massive silver chandeliers that unfolded from the ceiling were custom-designed Buck Rogers numbers with spheres and bowls and diagonal arms. Jazzy murals of dancers and musicians by Anthony Heinsbergen lined the walls.

Wayne McAllister and . . .

TOP AND ABOVE:
Guests danced to the world's top orchestras under the Jazz Age murals by Anthony Heinsbergen in the main ballroom. This room was directly inspired by the 1925 Exposition Internationale des Arts Decoratifs et Industriels Modernes in Paris. "That was our first start of Moderne," said McAllister.

ABOVE:
The menu for the famous dollar lunch offered continental cuisine by chef Alex Eggers. This is a menu that might be found at any fine hotel in America. Traditional Mexican dishes were rarely available.

Agua Caliente  51

The amenities of Las Vegas were invented at Agua Caliente. Lunch was a loss leader—only one dollar for soup, salad, entree, vegetable, dessert and coffee—Chef Alex Eggers created some of the most fantastic dishes for the famous patio lunch. One day the menu offered Lettuce Hearts with Mille Isle dressing, Capon Gumbo Manhattan or Cream of Almonds St. James, Baked Alaska Salmon with Lobster Sauce, Sliced Beef Tenderloin en Cassolette Point du Jour, Roast Loin of Pork with Dressing and Gooseberry Sauce or Stuffed Milk-Fed Chicken Madrilene, Mashed Creamed Potatoes Menagere, Buttered New Carrots and Garden Peas and Napoleon Slices or Caramel Ice Cream. Lunch was served on the patio daily and was accompanied by a floor show. Lavish entertainment filled the showroom. "We had all the top bands," remembered Wayne.

The casino was built without windows or clocks; the ornamental plasterwork ceilings masked catwalks used by security, including a young Art Linkletter. Even the eighty-five-foot campanile,

The ornamental plasterwork ceilings of the casino masked catwalks used by security.

184:—INTERIOR OF CASINO AND FAMOUS GOLD BAR.

AGUA CALIENTE, TIJUANA HOT SPRINGS, MEXICO.

Gold Bar at Agua Caliente.

a grand piece of sculpture in its own right—the logo, centerpiece and most remembered icon of the resort—served three functions: a bell tower, the beacon for the airstrip, and the sign entrance from the road. If you could find the sign, you could find the casino.

It was at this point that friends submitted Wayne and Corinne's design portfolio and the couple was offered attendance at the prestigious architecture school of the University of Pennsylvania. The Bauhaus school was still chiefly confined to Europe, and the McAllisters would have received a traditional education in the classical style. Architectural historian Alan Hess expressed the opinion that their unique style would have been "learned out of them" by the established school. "I was not a Modern architect at all at this point," McAllister said. "To be a Modern architect, you really needed the training that was given at the schools. I was not exposed to that."

In fact, few American architecture schools taught Modernism in 1928. It was a movement still in development in a handful of progressive architectural offices in Europe and America. In a few years, McAllister himself would contribute to that development.

The Agua Caliente partners and their backers in the Mexican government were planning two new resorts to rival the project, one in the seaside town of Rosarito and another in the hills of Monterrey, Mexico. The McAllisters were tapped to design both. In 1932 Wirt Bowman purchased land in Topo Chico, a suburb of Monterrey. It was located on a hilltop of a city that was attracting tourists from Texas and the Rio Grande Valley, and was to include a golf course and other amenities similar to Agua Caliente. Wayne and Corinne moved to Monterrey to supervise the $250,000 project and to serve as general contractors. However, when the plug was pulled on the project, they were the ones who had to explain the situation to an army of unemployed workers at the almost-completed hostelry.

"The Agua Caliente hotel and casino," according to the *San Diego Herald,* "were designed to attract a class of patron who now seek recreation in Europe on the Riviera and health at such famous European watering places as Carlsbad and Baden Baden." Almost

"AGUA CALIENTE HOTEL • OLD MEXICO"

Young performers like the dancer Margarita Cansino, who became Rita Hayworth, were discovered at Agua Caliente.

from the beginning, the hotel at Agua Caliente had a great pull on the motion picture community. An early menu drawn by bandleader Xavier Cugat depicts the Marx Brothers, Eddie Cantor, Laurel and Hardy, Joe E. Brown, and Raoul Walsh with his signature eye patch, cavorting with senoritas and mariachis. Charlie Chaplin attended the races with his friend Joseph M. Schenck, president of 20th Century Fox Studios. In 1929 Schenck, Al Jolson, Irving Berlin and Alexander Pantages were stockholders. In 1933 Schenck purchased a controlling share of the resort and was on its board of directors, along with Douglas Fairbanks and Jesse Lasky. The celebrity clientele became as much of a draw as Phar Lap or Seabiscuit on the track: Gary Cooper draping himself over the track rail; Jean Harlow taking a swing on the golf course, bell bottoms billowing; Bing Crosby and Clark Gable posing with their steeds; Howard Hughes casting films from a table full of young actresses. These images were published all over the world. At the end of 1934, Warner Brothers brought together Dolores del Rio, Busby Berkeley and the hotel for the motion picture *In Caliente.*

Unfortunately, in January 1935 President Lázaro Cárdenas of Mexico signed an executive order that outlawed gambling in Mexico. Two days later Baron Long ordered the complex closed and the grounds shuttered. "Prohibide Entrada" signs went up immediately and armed guards blocked all entrances. According to the *Los Angeles Herald Express,* "Here the blistering sun of tropical Mexico is wreaking havoc with greens fairways and tees. One week ago the water was turned off and even in this short time the course has withered to a sickly brown with only splotches of green to show what it once was. Another ten days and the gold course, which cost more than $200,000 to build, will be gone. Three months and it will not be so different from the barren hills that stretch away to the south . . . a million dollars worth of rare shrubs and beautiful trees are dying."

President Cárdenas's order determined the end, but the reasons for the very existence of Agua Caliente were already disappearing. In 1931 the state of Nevada passed legislation that allowed casino

Wayne and Corinne moved to Monterrey, Mexico, to supervise construction of the Topo Chico resort, a new hotel modeled on the success of Agua Caliente. It was never completed.

gambling. Liquor flowed freely again after Franklin Delano Roosevelt repealed the Eighteenth Amendment in 1933. And on December 25, 1934, the lavish Santa Anita racetrack opened in the Los Angeles suburb of Arcadia, California, changing the sport forever. President Cárdenas nationalized the assets of the Agua Caliente Company, and the hotel became an educational facility, a use it holds to this day. Much of the site remained intact until three fires in the 1960s and a major site-clearance program in 1975 wiped out everything but ruins of the spa, pool and minaret. The federal and state governments are working toward stabilization and preservation of the site.

For several years after the closure, rumors appeared in gossip pages and in the sports section about the reopening of Agua Caliente. There was much speculation that perhaps the track would come back or maybe the famous golf championship. A 1937 reopening attempt generated press but was short lived. The family of John Alessio fought for the return of land they claimed was seized illegally, and took over control of the Agua Caliente racetrack.

The 1938 season saw the triumphant wins of such racing legends as Seabiscuit and Phar Lap at the reinvigorated track. It continued to operate until 1972 when it was lost in a fire and replaced with a smaller facility that currently races championship greyhounds.

In 1982 Wayne and Corinne McAllister were given the key to the city of Tijuana in a ceremony honoring them as cocreators of one of the world's greatest resorts. They donated a set of original blueprints to the Tijuana Historical Society. Today, that same society is at the center of a Tijuana reinventing itself as a location of arts and culture in northern Mexico. Even though some see this period of American hedonism as shameful, there are others working on a conservation effort to stabilize and preserve the remains of the Agua Caliente site.

Cashing in on the public's interest in the playground of the stars, Warner Brothers cast Dolores del Rio as a dancer vacationing at the hotel in a scene from the Busby Berkley film *In Caliente,* released in 1935.

THE LADY IN RED

LYRIC BY MORT DIXON

MUSIC BY ALLIE WRUBEL

FIRST NATIONAL

presents

IN Caliente

WITH

DOLORES DEL RIO
PAT O'BRIEN
LEO CARILLO
EDWARD EVERETT HORTON
GLENDA FARRELL

DIRECTED BY
LLOYD BACON

DANCE NUMBERS CRE-
ATED AND DIRECTED BY
BUSBY BERKELEY

IN CALIENTE
THE LADY IN RED
TO CALL YOU MY OWN
LYRIC BY MORT DIXON
MUSIC BY ALLIE WRUBEL

MUCHACHA
LYRIC BY AL DUBIN
MUSIC BY HARRY WARREN

IN LOS ANGELES, IT'S THE
SHERATON
-TOWN HOUSE

Hotels
and Nightspots

U.S. GRANT HOTEL
U.S. GRANT HOTEL
USG
BARON LONG.
PRESIDENT
BROADWAY OPPOSITE THE PLAZA
SAN DIEGO, CAL.

Room

use · Los Angeles

Hotels and Nightspots

"Roosevelt was inaugurated March 4th, 1933," remembered McAllister, "and he was going to repeal the Volstead Act first by allowing beer." With Prohibition and the very foundation of Agua Caliente's success near repeal, Baron Long planned a great comeback for suds. Since breweries required specialized equipment that was not available in America, Long sent McAllister on an expedition to Nogales, Mexico, where he purchased the contents of the Wise Brewery and arranged to have them shipped north by rail. He also brought back retired brewmaster George Bode, who was thrilled to be brewing again after so many years.

BALBOA BREWING COMPANY

McAllister began the project with zero knowledge in brewing, but within a few months he became not only an expert in the business but also an innovator. Traditional breweries usually required five-story buildings but McAllister only had two stories of a former milk processing factory. Unable to rely on gravity to move the brew, he designed a series of pumps that accomplished this. The rapid success was so unusual that *Western Brewer* magazine disbelievingly wrote in asking for photos of the operation. Long and his investors founded the Ritz Brewing Company in the summer of 1933, then later changed the name to Balboa Brewing Company. Balboa was founded in a brick warehouse on Imperial Avenue in San Diego, California, and McAllister was named vice president.

In 1932 McAllister had finished plans for an addition on Long's U. S. Grant Hotel including an unusual parking structure that allowed visitors to enter in the center of the hotel. The new building also housed a grill and storefront lounge called the Rendezvous Room. Long asked McAllister to make an old-fashioned saloon with roast beef sandwiches and beer. They took a trip to Los Angeles

Before the repeal of prohibition, McAllister traveled to Mexico and learned to make beer from expert brewmasters not affected by the Eighteenth Amendment. Upon the completion of the Balboa Brewing Company in San Diego, Wayne inspects the first production in 1933.

for ideas and had the contract to sell their new Balboa Beer. This venture was so successful that soon other restaurants clamored for the beer.

Balboa was financed in shares of $100,000; Long owned 42 percent, McAllister had 15 percent and the last 43 percent was owned by a man named J. B. Simpson, who was involved because McAllister was supposed to be designing a house for him and was behind schedule because of the work he was doing on the brewery, so they gave him an option. Simpson became a booster in a new market: Los Angeles. They lost money shipping beer to Los Angeles, and by August 1933 they began an expansion plan in Los Angeles, taking over the long-defunct Mathie Brewery adjacent to the huge Pabst/Eastside plant. There was so much demand that by the following year the entire operation and its young vice president moved to Los Angeles. On New Year's Day 1934 Corinne and Wayne made their final trip out of San Diego to begin their new lives in Los Angeles. The couple climbed into Baron Long's Phaeton convertible cruiser and traveled up the coast to the elegant Biltmore Hotel, opposite Pershing Square Park in downtown Los Angeles, and set up residence in the hotel.

A few months prior to their arrival, a major earthquake shook Los Angeles and Long Beach, and the massive destruction prompted changes to building codes. In April, a building was purchased for the new Balboa plant: an un-reinforced masonry structure that was once a brewery was found, retrofitted and opened by September. The West Coast Brewing Association was formed, and McAllister became the director. Soon Balboa was thriving and became the tap beer of choice in Southern California. For a short time it ranked as the number-one best-selling beer in Southern California.

The demand was so high that Simpson decided to buy beer from other breweries and re-label it. A second hardship came when Pabst/Eastside plant and owner George Zobelein, whose facility was only a block away, wanted to close them down, and he convinced the

McAllister modernized Baron Long's U. S. Grant Hotel in San Diego, adding an innovative garage and motor court where guests arriving by car could enter the center of the hotel.

ABOVE:

Baron Long took over the lease on the Biltmore Hotel in 1934. His family would continue to operate it for decades. It became McAllister's home base in Los Angeles. McAllister moved into the Biltmore Hotel in 1934 and added bars on every floor, including the Biltmore Bowl and the Rendezvous Room.

RIGHT:

Cecil B. DeMille, Henry Fonda and Walt Disney are among the revelers at the IX Academy Awards, held at the Biltmore Bowl on March 4, 1937. The awards were held there sporadically from 1935 to 1942.

health department to crack down on places that served Balboa Beer. Soon the investors sold their shares and moved on.

BILTMORE HOTEL

Baron Long had acquired a lease to operate the Biltmore Hotel at the end of 1933. He would operate the hotel for decades. Though he kept an interest in Agua Caliente and the U. S. Grant Hotel, Long wanted to return to his old stomping grounds and expand his enterprise in the booming metropolis to the north. The Biltmore Hotel was Italian Renaissance in style and was designed by New York hotel architects Schultze and Weaver. It opened in 1923 and was the largest and

Ninth Annual Awards of Merit Presentation Dinner
Academy of Motion Picture Arts and Sciences
Biltmore Hotel   March 4 1937

The Biltmore Hotel
LOS ANGELES

among the most lavish hotels of the West. The original hotel boasted more than 1,100 rooms. It hosted everything from society tea dances to the Academy Awards. It was the first destination for traveling presidents when they visited the West Coast. "The original Biltmore in New York was financed by Cornelius Vanderbilt and J. P. Morgan, hence the name," according to Baron Bernard, the son of another Baron Long protégé, Edward S. Bernard, who spent many years as manager of the Los Angeles Biltmore Hotel. By December 1933, with the Depression in full swing, Long was able to secure a discounted lease on the venerable hostelry. His plan for making the hotel profitable again was simple: "We put cocktail bars on every floor,"

TOP:
Table tent from the Rendezvous
Room, "A Nightclub in the Afternoon."

ABOVE:
McAllister's Biltmore Bowl became
one of the most popular nightspots in
Los Angeles throughout the 1930s.

according to McAllister. With the repeal of the Volstead Act and the legalization of liquor effective beginning in 1934, Long had his favorite young architects and a plan to turn the hotel around. The restored hotel is City of Los Angeles Historic Cultural Monument #60 and continues to define the center of Downtown Los Angeles.

The Biltmore Hotel marked the social center of downtown Los Angeles in much the same way Long's U. S. Grant Hotel did in San Diego. In 1934 downtown Los Angeles was a thriving business and entertainment district and the nexus of one of the most extensive public transportation networks in the world.

McAllister and Long added a coffee shop, grill and two new nightclubs—the Biltmore Bowl and the Rendezvous Room—to the existing six restaurants. Adjoining these clubs were the Biltmore Lounge, the French Bar and the Cocktail Corner.

RENDEZVOUS ROOM

The Rendezvous Room was billed as "a nightclub in the afternoon," open from 1 to 7 p.m. Behind the existing Florentine arches, McAllister and Anthony Heinsbergen collaborated on an etched glass mural, *Wine, Women and Song,* culminating in a scene of nudes emerging from a cocktail mist and cavorting around a piano. The room offered dining and dancing, but the real star of the hotel was a lavish nightclub on the lower floor, the two-tiered Biltmore Bowl.

BILTMORE BOWL

The hotel was Italian Renaissance, according to McAllister. "We simply worked with what we had—beautiful stuff." Four months after Long proposed the idea, the Biltmore Bowl opened as "the world's largest nightclub," with terraced seating and a massive parquet dance floor. Opening night, April 5, 1934, found 1,200 patrons dining and dancing beneath the silk brocade and muraled vaults of the former Sala De Oro Ballroom. Brochures proclaimed it "the Rendezvous of the film folk of Hollywood," and the room hosted the Academy Awards ceremonies intermittently from 1935 to 1942. The proscenium

Twelve hundred revelers could fill the dance floor at the Biltmore Bowl. Big bands and radio broadcasts originated from the massive club.

was carved with the same delicate scallops and cartouches seen at Agua Caliente. Corinne designed the Biltmore Bowl with its terraced balconies, which were not allowed under the Los Angeles building code. Wayne and Corinne had to bring a sample of the treated wood to the planning department to prove that it would withstand the load requirements.

The five-dollar opening-night ticket included champagne and a night of entertainment from Hal Roberts and his orchestra. The biggest film stars mingled with dancers, society folk and music lovers to hear the big bands of Harry James and Jimmie Grier. The largest radio station in Los Angeles, KFI, broadcasted the shows nationally. The 140-foot-long room of the Bowl had a ceiling with murals by Anthony Heinsbergen, and an arched colonnade ran its length. The room had no central support columns and offered clear views of and for its 1,200 patrons. "Every table is ringside," according to another brochure. After the Screen Actors Guild threw a lavish ball the day before Thanksgiving that first year, attended by James Cagney, Claudette Colbert, Edward G. Robinson, George Raft, Ann Sothern and Joe E. Brown, the Bowl became a top nightclub in a downtown that was at the height of its zeitgeist.

PIG 'N WHISTLE

As the McAllisters settled into life at the Biltmore, they added a coffee shop, a grill and a candy counter, featuring the chocolates of the Pig 'n Whistle. J. H. Gage founded the Pig 'n Whistle candy company simultaneously in Los Angeles and San Francisco in 1908. A bright young manager named Sidney Hoedemaker expanded it into a restaurant operation by the 1920s. McAllister went on to design many restaurants for Hoedemaker. His reputation for Agua Caliente and his successful work at the Biltmore brought McAllister almost immediate attention in the Los Angeles dining industry. Baron Long was "the dean of hotel men and restaurateurs among the local fraternity" and introduced McAllister to these folks, where he established relationships that would last for decades.

The cocktail lounges and hotel nightspots that the McAllisters designed in this period became increasingly more experimental. "I think I should retrace something now. When we were designing the cafe and casino at [Agua] Caliente, this was the year of the World's Fair [1925 Exposition Internationale des Arts Decoratifs et Industriels Modernes] in Paris. That's where the real Modern movement was exemplified; that's when it came out. The interiors of the casino building were all designed in the Spanish tradition, but we decided, because we got all the stuff from the World's Fair, that we would

Olvera Street runs through the historic El Pueblo de Los Angeles monument, the birthplace of Los Angeles. Civic activist Christine Sterling brought in McAllister to design a cafe in the old Mexican style that would be compatible with her vision of a themed village. Cafe Caliente opened in 1934.

Hotel owner Thomas Hull commissioned McAllister to work on his hotels, including the Hollywood Plaza, Hollywood Roosevelt and a series of El Rancho motor hotels.

change our concept of the cafe. So even though we had drawn it the other way, we stopped and changed it. We lowered the ceiling and went with our version of things we saw in the plates and drawings and information that came out of Paris. My decorator [Anthony Heinsbergen] brought back influences having to do with Moderne, as they called it. That was the Zigzag Moderne style, which we did in the dining room; that was our first start of Moderne. Then of course, architecturally speaking, Spanish was out in Los Angeles and Moderne was in, so contemporary was what we were doing."

HOLLYWOOD ROOSEVELT HOTEL

CINEGRILL

A week after the Biltmore Bowl opened downtown, veteran hotelier Thomas E. Hull, owner of the Senator Hotel in Sacramento, the California in Fresno and the Plaza and Mayfair hotels in Los Angeles, acquired the lease on the Hollywood Roosevelt, a twelve-story luxury hotel built in 1927 in the Spanish Colonial Revival style. Hull hired McAllister to add a coffee shop and a restaurant, and to modernize the public spaces of the hotel. The showstopper would be a state-of-the-art nightclub called the Cinegrill, with its main entrance on Hollywood Boulevard, opposite Grauman's Chinese Theatre. The portal was movie-set Moderne. The wide chrome-plated door was shiny and flat, and the entrance was faced with enameled plum terra-cotta from the Gladding McBean Tile Company. Flanking the door were mullion-less glass cases, often filled with champagne bottles. The door featured an etched mural that would have been entirely appropriate for a Busby Berkeley musical. The mural showed wildly gesturing dancers gliding across a celluloid strip with musical notes riding over the backs of others. At the base was a seated young couple observing the scene. A metallic "Cinegrill" sign was positioned above it all, backlit by a fluorescent-glass panel. Brazilian rosewood lined the walls, and Wayne and Corinne collaborated with artist Maurice

MURALSCOPE
Hollywood Roosevelt Hotel
Hollywood, Calif.

ABOVE:
The Hollywood Boulevard entrance to the Cinegrill nightclub in the Roosevelt Hotel. The modernized facade was draped in high-gloss purple and stainless steel.

BELOW AND RIGHT:
Wayne and Corinne collaborated with the artist Maurice Trapet to design a dizzying photomural wallcovering featuring "every star from John Bunny to present-day favorites."

The pool and new guest wing at the Hollywood Roosevelt Hotel was added by architect Frank Green, with McAllister as consulting architect. It has recently been restored and its Tropicana bar is flourishing.

Trapet to design a dizzying photomural wall covering featuring "every star from John Bunny to present-day favorites," as hyped by a fan magazine. The successful club became a favorite romantic rendezvous for Clark Gable and Carole Lombard and was a haven for writers, including Ernest Hemingway and F. Scott Fitzgerald. Hull and McAllister installed similar lounges in his Mayfair and Hollywood Plaza hotels. Fifteen years later, after McAllister had designed a series of El Rancho hotels for Hull, he was called in to consult on an addition to the Roosevelt. This was designed in the South American luxury resort pattern and was nestled in a tropical garden setting with a profusion of island flowers and dramatic planting.

Wayne McAllister and . . .

BELOW:
The thirteen-story red brick and cast-stone Town House Hotel was built in 1928 by Norman W. Alpaugh as an apartment building.

ABOVE:
McAllister added a side entrance to the Zebra Room nightclub. It was clad in mirror-patterned marble with a Streamline Moderne entrance canopy faced in scalloped stainless steel. A galloping neon zebra was stationed nearby. The room was an instant success and attracted more of the nightclub-hopping film crowd.

TOWN HOUSE HOTEL

Just outside downtown Los Angeles, the thirteen-story red brick and cast-stone Town House Hotel was built as an apartment building in 1928 by Norman W. Alpaugh. The site is on a bend in the newly completed road and sits across the street from Bullocks Wilshire, the most stylish department store in town. In the 1930s this chic neighborhood, adjacent to Lafayette Park, featured a seven-acre park and lake with snazzy boutiques, restaurants and a lavish movie palace. In 1937 the apartment building was converted into a luxury hotel. McAllister was given the job of adding a nightclub and lounge with an exotic theme.

ZEBRA ROOM

By December 1937 the Zebra Room opened its doors onto Wilshire Boulevard. McAllister added a side entrance clad in mirror-patterned marble with a Streamline Moderne entrance canopy faced in scalloped stainless steel. A galloping neon zebra was stationed nearby. The room was an instant success and attracted more of the nightclub-hopping film crowd.

The Zebra Room was a well-proportioned and lively room with vertical blond wood dividers and grilles flanking planters of live cacti throughout the space. The theme was set from the exterior entrance where a rubber mat made to imitate the skin of a zebra

appeared beneath patrons' feet. The room had a color scheme of off-white and black with a coral ceiling. The walls were festooned with fantastic murals featuring wild zebras racing through the Serengeti with playful imbibing monkeys nearby—perhaps a play on the immensely popular Cocoanut Grove nightclub at the Ambassador Hotel just down the street. Every chair was upholstered in an arresting zebra-design leather. Square tables with tabletop lamps and zebra wood inlays continued the motif, as did custom inverted zebra-head mugs, which served the hotels specialty cocktails. The room was modified many times but lasted at the hotel into the 1960s.

The Zebra Room interior was a riot of zebra stripes in the upholstery, woodwork and even the entrance floor mat.

CAPE COD GRILL

Thomas Hull also added a fine dining restaurant called the Cape Cod Grill that specialized in "New England dishes in a New England atmosphere." The new spot was a setting of oak beams, antique pewter and cheery red-checked cloths on maple tables. Of course, the menu featured clam chowder and apple pie with a "Boston tang."

LANAI ROOMS

A decade later, McAllister was called back to the Town House Hotel, which had recently been purchased by his friend Conrad Hilton, to add sixteen garden rooms with walls of glass and innovative sliding glass doors to the evolving hostelry. This low-slung wing wrapped around the hotel pool and rooms, which had private lanai patios called the Lanai Suites. A new undulating brick wall enclosed this section and became the new center of the hotel.

Of interest was a new type of aluminum window sash that enabled guests to slide back one-third of the glass wall without

RIGHT:
The Town House lanai is a sunny oasis of leisure relaxation hidden just off busy Wilshire Boulevard.

OPPOSITE:
The spire of the art deco Bullocks Wilshire Department Store rises behind the pool at the Town House Hotel.

effort. All units were wired for televisions and radios as part of the standard equipment.

Each suite was divided by the same egg-crate wooden walls that were utilized later at the Sands in Las Vegas. The effect was astonishing. The tropical landscaping and Bermuda modern design transported guests to a resort even if they were mere feet from the bustle of a busy boulevard. Below the pool was a viewing area known as the Underwater Room where one could watch friends through portholes as they swam beneath the surface.

In 1993 the hotel was saved from demolition and now serves as affordable housing in Los Angeles. It is City of Los Angeles Historic Cultural Monument #576.

The pool and Lanai Suites at the Town House Hotel were described as "Bermuda modern" and presaged McAllister's work at the Sands Hotel in Las Vegas.

There is evidence to suggest that McAllister was called on to install casino gambling in the historic Arrowhead Springs Resort in the San Bernardino Mountains about an hour east of Los Angeles. The resort dates to the nineteenth century. Designed by Gordon Kaufmann, the current building opened in 1939 and was heavily remodeled by architect Paul R. Williams, whose Hollywood Regency makeover, with its oversized molding and striped wallpaper predicting Williams's work at the Beverly Hills Hotel of 1947.

McAllister had connections to each of the string of owners of the hotel. In 1939 a majority share was purchased by Joseph Schenck, an owner of Agua Caliente and an epic gambler. Schenck was in the news after an illegal gambling casino was discovered in his home in 1935. According to the *Los Angeles Times* in 1941, Al Wertheimer testified that he took over the Sunset Boulevard home of Schenck and turned it into a casino without the knowledge of the millionaire film executive. "[He] complained because we tore down a couple of walls to make room for a roulette wheel," said Wertheimer. Wertheimer was also involved in illegal gambling at the Dunes in Palm Springs and at the Clover Club on Sunset Boulevard along with the film director Raoul Walsh, an Agua Caliente regular during Schenck's time. Schenck and another legendary gambler, Billy Wilkerson, the nightclub impressario behind Ciro's and founder of *The Hollywood Reporter,* collaborated on a number of failed gambling projects. Wayne remembered that Wilkerson started illegal gambling in the Clover Club and also put in illegal gambling in Arrowhead Springs, probably during Schenk's time. Interestingly, Thomas Hull of Hull Hotels bought Arrowhead Springs in 1946, after McAllister completed his El Rancho Vegas project. In 1949, two years after McAllister's work on the Town House, Conrad Hilton purchased Arrowhead Springs through Joseph Drown, as a personal purchase not related to his corporation.

The Clover Club was a bustling nightspot, but also a den of illicit gambling above Hollywood's Sunset strip.

"THE HOLLYWOOD" . . . Sunset Boulevard at Cahuenga

Welcome to Simon's

Hody's
RESTAURANT
FOOD TO TAKE HOME
FOUNTAIN
Hody's
Family Restaurants
of Southern California
HODY'S
CHARCOAL BROILED STEAKS

Drive-Ins

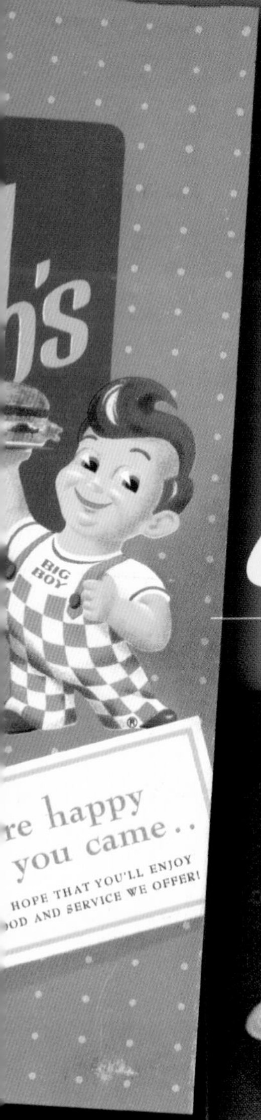

re happy
you came...

HOPE THAT YOU'LL ENJOY
OOD AND SERVICE WE OFFER!

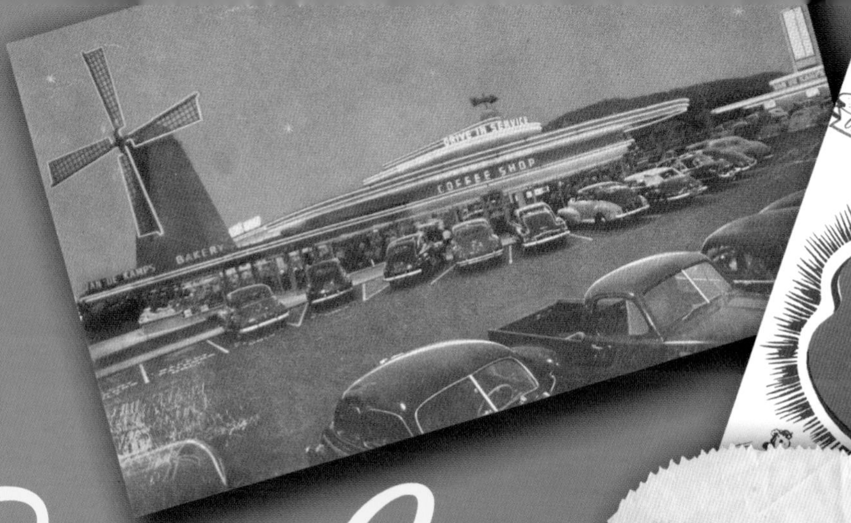

ALL OVER THE LOS ANGELES FUN MAP...
YOU'LL FIND FINE FOOD AT

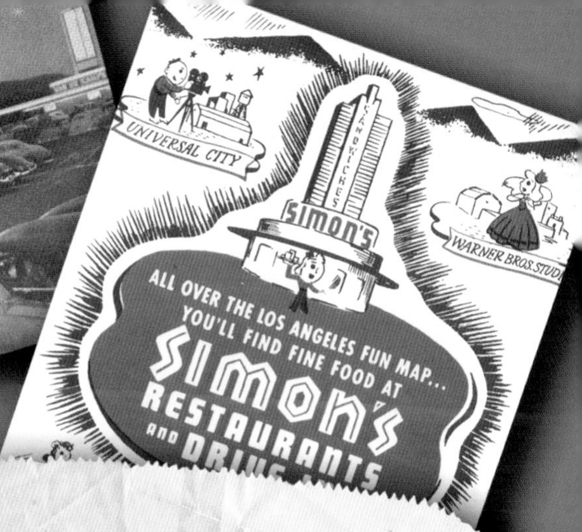

Simon's
RESTAURANTS
and DRIVE

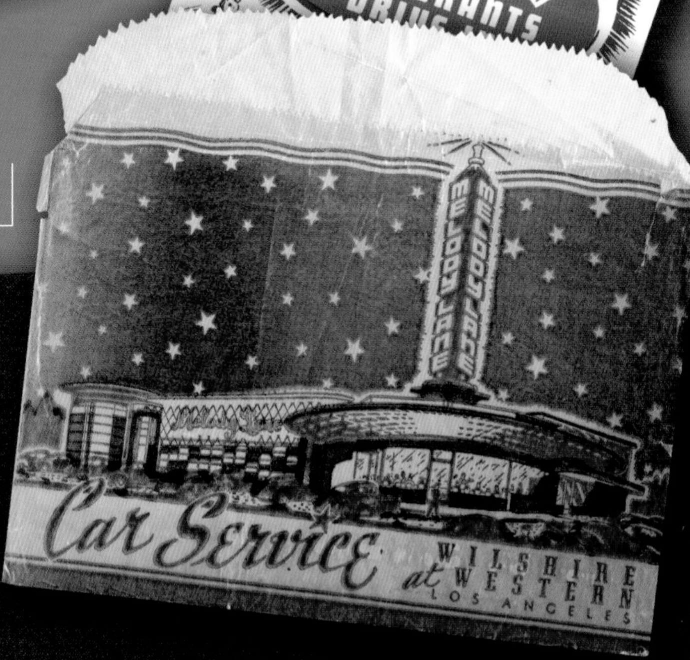

UNIVERSAL CITY

WARNER BROS. STUDIO

Car Service

WILSHIRE
at WESTERN
LOS ANGELES

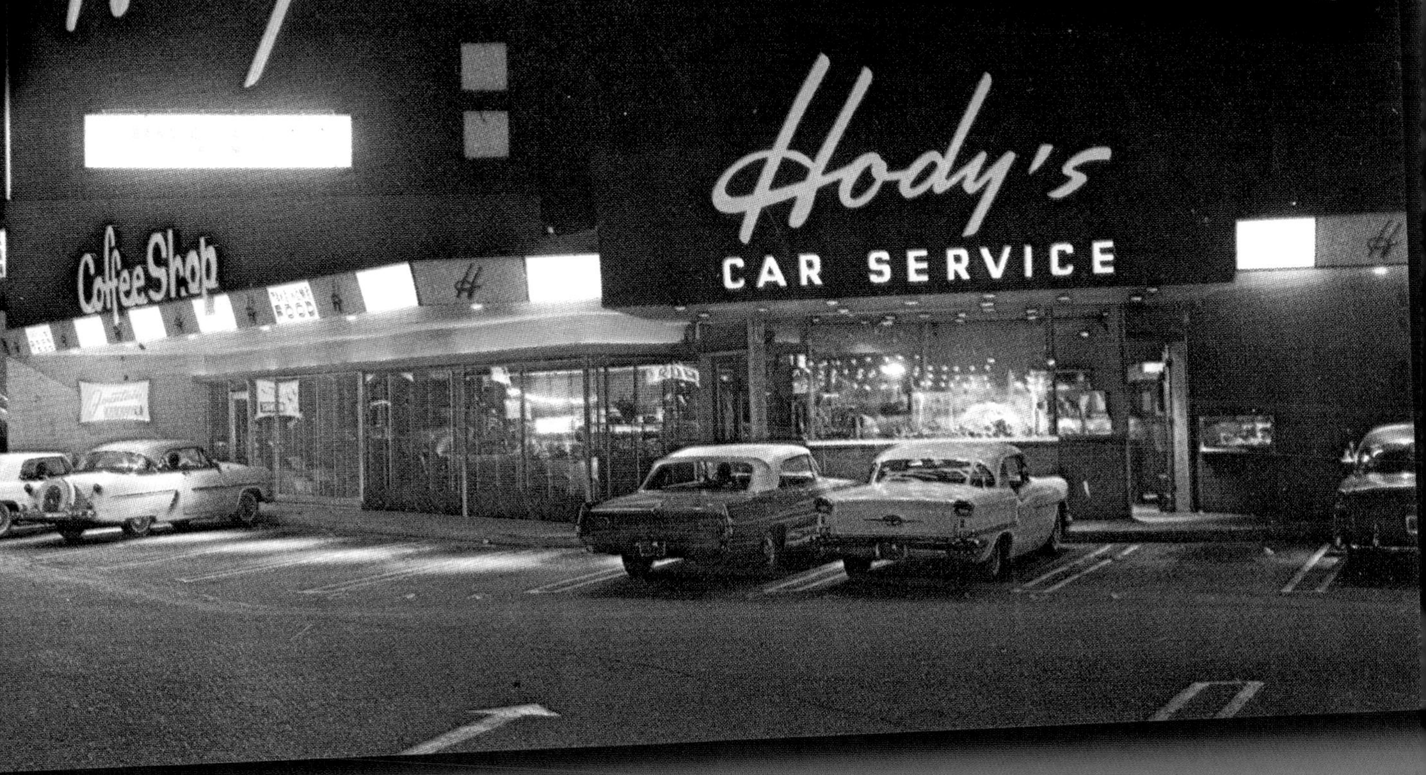

Hody's

Coffee Shop

Hody's
CAR SERVICE

The first drive-in restaurants in America were sandwich and barbecue stands in arid climates that permitted outdoor dining year-round. The Pig Stands in the South and the Texan Harry Carpenter's chain in Southern California were basically simple kitchens surrounded by a counter. Some of the all-night operations didn't even have doors. At the end of the 1920s the vernacular stands had become octagonal wedding cake assemblages laden with hand-lettered cards for hot apple pie and chili con carne. Architectural historian Alan Hess observed that McAllister "pulled the somewhat crude vernacular expressions of the drive-in restaurant into a unified, sophisticated, and

Simon's was one of the biggest drive-in chains. Their slogan was "A Simon's wherever you turn."

**LOCATIONS OF
S I M O N ' S**
Drive-Ins

WILSHIRE AND FAIRFAX
WILSHIRE AND HOOVER
EXPOSITION AND FIGUEROA
SUNSET AND HIGHLAND
OLYMPIC AND SOTO
WILSHIRE AND LINDEN
WASHINGTON AND GRAND
FLORENCE AND ATLANTIC
FIVE POINTS, EL MONTE

utterly Modern whole," and he could "take that vernacular form and fine tune it. He made it more sophisticated and added architectural values, and qualities." Architects KEM Weber, R. M. Schindler and even Ludwig Mies Van Der Rohe attempted to design drive-in restaurants. Few were built and none were as successful as McAllister's. "He was doing it better than anyone else in the country," according to Hess. "These were arguably the most radically Modern buildings ever constructed in the United States. No other buildings were shaped so effectively by technology—by the automobile. No modern building unified function, advertising and urban presence more effectively. To make a relatively small building visible to customers from far down the street, the entire building was conceived as a sign to attract customers."

The operations fit Los Angeles particularly well, a mobile city filling with automobiles, spreading out into the suburbs and with a climate that predicated an indoor/outdoor lifestyle. Some of the twenty-four-hour restaurants shunned not only locks but also front doors altogether. McAllister came up with an appropriate architecture: he had to reinvent architecture for the car city.

SIMON'S DRIVE-INS

In Roosevelt-era Los Angeles, drive-in restaurants were nearly as ubiquitous as drive-thru restaurants are today. Whole legions of carhops staffed these all-day, all-night dining spots, and they became beacons for workers and young couples looking for an inexpensive night on the town. One of the biggest chains, Simon's (1935–42), had the slogan "A Simons wherever you turn."

The operation was owned by Bill Simon, a gambling buddy of restaurateurs Harry Carpenter and "Rusty" McDonnell. Simon started with a chain of dairy lunches, a type of lunch counter, in Chicago. In the 1920s he moved to Los Angeles with his brothers Abe and Mike Lyman. Mike took over the venerable Al Levy's tavern restaurants. McAllister remembered his brother Abe Lyman. "He was a famous bandleader of the big band era. They called him the Irish Thrush—he was Jewish."

A carhop on the menu cover of Simon's Drive-In. Carhop drive-ins were once as prevalent as drive-thru restaurants today.

McAllister met Simon when he was asked to install cocktail lounges in some of his restaurants as he had done at the Biltmore Hotel. The brothers owned about fifty restaurants, dairy lunches and drive-ins, according to McAllister. "I designed them all." McAllister recalled:

When I joined [Simon] he was in the restaurant business and had all these dairy lunches. Then he decided a year or two later that he would follow a new trend that had been started by a couple of other restaurateurs that had put in these drive-ins. He got together with me and said "Wayne, I know damn well these guys are spending too much money on their buildings. I think we can do it for a lot less money." He gave me a budget of $6,500 to build and equip a drive-in restaurant. He had a bet with them that we could do it, and they had a bet that we couldn't do it. The first one we did was at Wilshire and Fairfax, and we got it done for $6,500. The whole concept of the building was different from theirs. They built a masonry building and then put a tower on it. What I designed was a flat dish supported mainly on steel columns. I just filled it in and put a tower on it so that the flat dish overhead came out far enough to cover the first row of cars. The others had nothing like that, so we innovated the circular drive-in.

Simon's was a neon oasis on the wet streets of noir Los Angeles. In *The Little Sister,* Raymond Chandler decried the drive-ins as "sleazy hamburger joints that look like palaces under the colors, the circular drive-ins, as gay as circuses."

Simon's opened in 1935, looking like a fantastic Buck Rogers rocket ship hovering above the corner of Wilshire and Fairfax. The collection of bold, simple shapes and brilliant colors was accentuated in the evening by light. The effervescent glow of red neon tied the whole composition together like the perfect movie set. Five years later this tiny stand would be overshadowed by the marble and mosaic May Company department store across the street. Architect A. C. Martin's masterpiece was saved and incorporated into the Los Angeles County Museum of Art in 1999. The drive-in was demolished in 1955. Like many small drive-ins of the '30s, it was replaced by a full-service

Simon's Drive-In, Hollywood. The heyday of the drive-in was before the start of WWII. "Maybe they're saving on tires. I don't know," said owner Bill Simon when asked where his customers went for the duration. "I guess that's war."

restaurant. In this case, Simon's was replaced by the striking Romeo's Times Square, designed by Louis Armet and Eldon Davis, the masters of the googie coffee shop. But McAllister's design for the first Simon's would "launch a series of intrinsically influential and ultimately iconic designs that reshaped the American landscape and allowed the American public to live easily with the auto," according to Hess.

TOP:
Presentation drawing for the Roberts Project.

———————

ABOVE:
Matchbook detail from the Wich Stand Drive-In, Los Angeles, shows the drama of the tiny stand.

———————

OPPOSITE:
The blazing neon tower of the Wich Stand on Slauson Avenue really stood out in the Los Angeles landscape. The chain was founded by Glenn and Lewis Burford in 1937.

The drive-in trade was probably at its peak when Pearl Harbor was attacked at the end of 1941. The following month three new Simon's drive-ins were completed in Los Angeles. With the population changing focus and gas and tire rationing kicking in, spontaneous visits to places like Simon's became less frequent. In January 1942 columnist Tom Treanor quipped, "Every time a tire blows, Mr. Simon loses one potential drive-in customer. If it makes you or me shudder every time we slam on the brakes and make our own tires squeal, imagine the state of Mr. Simon's nerves. It makes him shudder every time anyone puts on the brakes and makes any tires squeal." Simon responded in kind: "I don't know why, but ever since the blackouts, the late-night business has never been good. Maybe people just don't feel like going out at night or maybe they're saving on tires. I don't know. I guess that's war."

WICH STAND DRIVE-INS

The Wich Stand was a chain founded by Glenn and Lewis Burford in 1937. The name was a play on "sandwich stand" and operated from two locations in Los Angeles. The first, at Figueroa and Florence, adjoined a zeppelin-shaped cocktail lounge, the second was at Slauson and Overhill and was the northern terminus of the auto-cruising circuit in the '50s and '60s. The Beach Boys even recorded an unreleased cut in 1966 called "Wich Stand" with Capitol Records. The pylon at the Wich Stand was one of the most remarkable ever created. It had a pierced circular fin protruding from stepped neon and rose some twenty feet above the roof.

ROBERTS DRIVE-INS

The Roberts drive-ins were some of the most elaborate designs of this period—especially in their neon sign displays. "Of course, to make a billboard out of it, to put a tower on it, was the natural thing to do. The towers I designed had louvers and lit neon tubes behind each louver, so it was luminescent without having any neon showing," said McAllister.

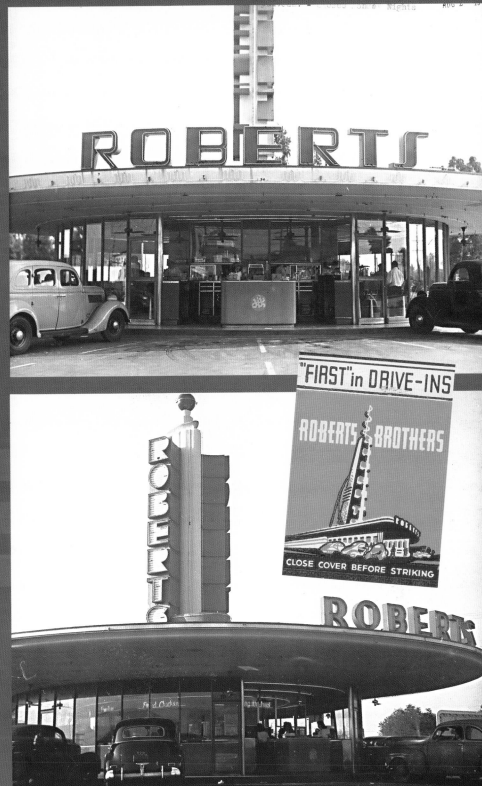

"FIRST" in DRIVE-INS

ROBERTS BROTHERS

CLOSE COVER BEFORE STRIKING

As the Roberts chain grew, such amenities as booth seating and jukeboxes were added.

Melody Lane

RESTAURANT · COCKTAIL ROOM · CAR SERVICE

Pig'n Whistle Candies and Pastries

WILSHIRE BOULEVARD AT WESTERN AVENUE

Los Angeles

PIG 'N WHISTLE RESTAURANT/MELODY LANE/HODY'S

For decades, the Pig 'n Whistle restaurants remained innovators in Los Angeles. In 1934 McAllister remodeled their stand-alone candy counter in the Biltmore Hotel and began a long relationship with founder Sidney Hoedemaker. The Pig 'n Whistle developed Melody Lane (c. 1939; see additional data on page 114), which eventually became Hody's (c. 1952; see page 92), and McAllister was there through it all. The Melody Lane at Wilshire and Western was a spectacular five-room operation combining a drive-in, coffee shop, candy shop and cocktail lounge called the Starlite Room. This composition of curves is one of the first designs to blend the Streamline with the emerging late Moderne style. The now-familiar rounded canopy rides on one end while the volume connecting the two halves of the restaurant is etched with diamond shapes of button-tufted upholstery. "The entire building was bathed in neon for a 'world of tomorrow' look," according to historian Jim Heimann.

The coffee shop was finished in peach, turquoise and eight shades of tan and brown. Historian Jim Heimann describes the interior: "The imposing cocktail lounge was the restaurant's centerpiece. The Starlite Room was built around the theme of the zodiac and had walls covered with flocked silk rayon. Hassocks replaced chairs and a 'record operator' would play requests on a stand flanked by copper backed, peach colored mirrors. The seats at the bar were joined by several bar stools that would accommodate three people on 'bar couches.' The shallow dome above the bar was painted with an exact reproduction of the stars, planets and constellations as they were in place above Los Angeles in February of 1942, while a translucent globe depicting the zodiac rotated in the center above a pyramid of cocktail glasses. The carpet was dyed in fluorescent colors and black lit."

Amoebas, lozenges and egg-crate shapes marked many of the new Late Moderne commercial buildings. Icons of the style were Wurdeman

OPPOSITE:
Melody Lane menu cover.

ABOVE:
The entrance to the Starlite Room at Melody Lane. This room was a Day-Glo study in astronomy with a mural of the night skies as they appeared over Los Angeles in February 1942.

Starlite Room

Melody Lane

MELODY LANE

COFFEE SHOP

Melody Lane

WILSHIRE BOULEVARD
AT WESTERN · LOS ANGELES

and Becket's Bullocks Pasadena, the postwar theaters of S. Charles Lee and a number of Sears stores designed by Stiles O. Clements.

Eventually, Melody Lane was renamed Hody's. Another one opened in 1953 at La Brea and Rodeo in Los Angeles. This was a co-venture with architect Lewis Wilson. It seated 125 and was a contemporary California modern building, with brick, wood and glass walls featuring subtropical plantings and an overhanging roof.

Holy Land author and Lakewood city historian D. J. Waldie was a frequent diner at Hody's as a child. He writes: "Lakewood Boulevard at Candlewood Street in Lakewood Center—Hody's Family Restaurant in 1952 was caramel and tangerine stucco on the outside and walnut veneer and red vinyl in the half-dark interior. Somewhere even darker, where I never went, there was a cocktail lounge."

He talks of the terrifying clown masks and the dried fish entombed in resin booth dividers. The experience was overpowering

to the young Waldie. "I have no memory of the food, except the intense tomato redness of the viscous French dressing Hody's served on salads. It was astringent and too sweet, rather like our lives then."

HERBERT'S DRIVE-INS

The Herbert's chain (c. 1936), founded by Dr. Herbert T. Movius, was especially adept at securing prime locations for their drive-ins: Wilshire at La Cienega, Ventura at Laurel Canyon. McAllister remembered,

ABOVE:
Contractors study McAllister's drive-in plans.

RIGHT:
Robert C. Wian's Bob's Big Boy empire started behind the counter of this first ten-stool diner in Glendale, c. 1936. Big Boy would go on to become one of the largest restaurant chains in the country.

"Each time we got a bigger lot in a better location, we could do more business and expand the size so that we ended up with an oval-shaped building that had probably fifty stools; twenty-five on each side of the counter in addition to the carhop service." One of their first stores was at the southeast corner of Beverly and Fairfax, adjacent to the beloved Los Angeles Farmers Market. Gilmore Field and Gilmore Stadium flanked the eastern edge of the property. In 1950 Dr. Movius was bought out for $100,000. The baseball field and stadium followed, and soon CBS Television City appeared on the site.

McDONNELL'S DRIVE-INS

McAllister designed several restaurants for another popular chain. In 1938 he did the first of several large McDonnell's drive-ins. These were elaborately themed stores, and the first was done in the oddly pervasive American Colonial Revival theme. A cupola-topped, two-story wood-sided plantation house with white pillars and shutters rose in the dairy ranches of South Gate. The sides of the building were faced with rough stone on which hung the neon signs for McDonnell's Plantation. It was just down the street from the large new General Motors plant and its 4,000 employees. Portions of this restaurant survive today as the Elizabeth Bakery. In collaboration with Bill Simon, a "super" McDonnell's opened in Glendale at San Fernando and Sonora, adjacent to the Grand Central Air terminal. "Before they've even finished building, Sonora is expected to be closed by the army," said columnist Tom Treanor in February 1942. When asked how one designer could so easily switch from historical Mount Vernon to the latest Moderne styles, McAllister replied, "Just the times, that's all. Nobody sticks with anything very long."

VAN DE KAMP'S

In 1915 Lawrence L. Frank and Theodore Van de Kamp came to Los Angeles and opened a small shop in downtown Los Angeles, selling potato chips made nearby. Two years later the partners opened their first Van de Kamp's Holland Dutch Bakery retail store, and by 1919 opened their first restaurant, or "bakery lunch." In 1931 they built a massive plant, the "Taj Mahal of bakeries," and soon opened a show-place retail store, bakery, drive-in and coffee shop.

Adjacent to their massive concrete Flemish-style bakery, the company opened a traditional-style bake shop, selling their Van de Kamp's Holland Dutch brand to showcase the goods baked next door. In 1940 McAllister was called on to expand and make the showcase store stand out. He added two oval-shaped buildings to the original hexagon-shaped bakery cafe with the Dutch windmill.

ABOVE:

A menu illustration of McDonnell's Plantation, South Gate, shows its Mount Vernon roots. This is one of the only drive-ins from this period to survive.

—————

BELOW:

The windmill rises above McDonnell's Rancho on Highway 99 in Glendale. This location was across from Glendale's Grand Central Airport.

McDonnell's *Rancho*
Located in West Glendale on
San Fernando Boulevard
Adjacent the Grand Central Airport

By day and by night, cars clamor for a spot under the neon-ringed canopy of Van de Kamp's Drive-In.

He added a drive-in, expanded the existing coffee shop and created a neon-ringed Streamline Moderne wonderland that was a crucial building in explaining Los Angeles to the established architectural circles/journals of the East. The twin drive-in was a complex series of neon and stucco rings stretched wide around a glass dining area punctuated with glass brick in smooth plaster walls. These drive-ins "may be the model of a future architecture," wrote architecture critic Henry Russell Hitchcock.

Outside of Neutra's work and that of his group, most of the interesting things are, so far as I could discover, effectively anonymous. I mean the drive-ins, of which there are several good examples on Sunset Boulevard and perhaps the finest of all—despite its unfortunate trademark windmill—at the corner of Glendale and San Fernando. These represent a very model of what exposition or resort architecture ought to be, light, gay, open, well executed and designed to be as effective by night as by day. . . . Nothing in the East compares with the best things of this sort in Los Angeles.

5555 Wilshire Blvd.

ONTRA CAFETERIA

The Ontra Cafeteria chain was well established in Los Angeles when they called on McAllister to add two additional stores. The first, in the Miracle Mile shopping district opened in 1945. The second, located in the Crenshaw district, was a $3 million project that opened four years later—a feeding factory with a capacity of six hundred. By 1961 more than one million people dined at Ontra annually. Both of these stores were in the late Moderne style with a largely blank facade. They were geometric and asymmetrical, and defined by very large neon signs draped across their elevation. The interiors continued the look with wedge-shaped soffits, simple lighting fixtures and box-frame details.

BOB'S BIG BOY

Bob's Big Boy is a legendary California-born chain founded in 1936 by Robert C. Wian. The restaurant, known for its chubby pompadoured mascot, debuted the world's first triple-decker burger. Bob Wian would go on to become the mayor of Glendale, the youngest in that city's history.

"I met Bob at the little ten-stool place in Glendale." McAllister remembered, "He was right there in the kitchen working . . . and he told me what he would like to do next door. That's when we came up with the strictly drive-up carhop service to cars. It had no seating." Bob's Glendale was a twin drive-in with a generous overhang and tower with vertical neon blades following a rounded corner that allowed the signage to be seen from two directions. Resting against this composition was a grimacing neon Big Boy holding a burger aloft and almost twice the size of the entire building. Neon Bob's script flowed across both facades and the words "original double deck hamburger" appeared lit from behind with halo neon. Even immediately following the war this was a class operation. Flagstone walls with integrated planters near the top brought this futuristic visage back to earth. The underside of the canopy was covered in multiple layers of neon. The goal was always the same: "To make a relatively small building visible to customers from far down the street," according to historian Alan Hess. "The entire building was conceived as a sign to attract customers."

Bob's was an early proponent of the total design movement. There was completeness to the design at Bob's. For decades, everything from the menus to the waxed paper wrappers to the larger-than-life Big Boy statues followed the same graphic package set forth in those first few stores. "Bob was always very much involved in planning with me," said McAllister. "He had his own ideas about kitchen layout because he built his Big Boy [sandwich] differently than the other people did. He imposed a lot of extra work by having a three decker [burger]."

OPPOSITE, BOTTOM:
The Ontra Cafeteria chain was a well-established operation when McAllister was called in to add two locations.

ABOVE:
A massive neon Big Boy being lowered into place at Bob's Drive-In #1 at 910 East Colorado in Glendale in 1947.

The first Bob's in Glendale after its neon makeover.

EXIT

THE ORIGINAL

BURBANK

SAN FERNANDO ROAD

115 W. BROADWAY

900 E. COLORADO

Bob's

GLENDALE

famous for

ORIGINAL
DOUBLE-DECK
HAMBURGERS

TOP, LEFT:
Bob Wian (right) with a group of carhops at the remodeled Glendale location. In 1947 he became the youngest mayor in the history of the city of Glendale.

BOTTOM, LEFT:
Vintage menus can be like treasure maps. This 1949 Bob's menu shows not only the locations of the first two stores but includes an architectural rendering as well.

In August 1949 work started on Bob's Big Boy in Burbank, near Toluca Lake. Locals Ward Albert and Scott McDonald owned the land at Riverside Drive and Rose, and with Wian, hired McAllister to design their showplace drive-in. In 1998 the *Los Angeles Times* proclaimed that the "crescent of concrete and glass . . . so swallows its stretch of Riverside Drive there's no telling whether you're inside or out." The composition is still energetic with its hybrid Late Moderne style. The interior expanded on the straightforward diner-type operation with indoor plantings; neon hidden in the layered soffits; birds-of-paradise growing out of curved countertops; and rounded corners with curving seat backs in wood grain Formica, tiled walls and striped asphalt flooring. The real action, however, was in the drive-in at the rear. Chris Hansen was a vice president at Bob's and worked his way up from dishwasher to lot man to security at the Burbank drive-in. "We were as popular as Elvis," Hansen said. "You couldn't get near the place on Friday nights. It seemed like everybody in town stopped at Bob's that night. They were attracted by the good food, gorgeous waitresses and the action. There was always something going on at Bob's Big Boy."

"When you're designing something, you don't look back at anything else. It flows from your ideas, not from what you did before," said McAllister. "But naturally, what you did before is in the background, isn't it? You certainly don't want to just repeat what you did before. The elements come together to make a building function the way you want them to function and then you make them look the way you want them to look. And it simply comes out that way."

Today, the Burbank restaurant is restored and honored as a State of California point of historical interest. "That restaurant is the

HOME OF THE
BIG BOY HAMBURGERS

Bob's

Famous for
HAMBURGERS
CHILI • STEAKS
THICK MALTS
THIN PANCAKES

3 Locations

115 W. BROADWAY
AND
900 E. COLORADO
GLENDALE
•
624 E. SAN FERNANDO RD.
BURBANK

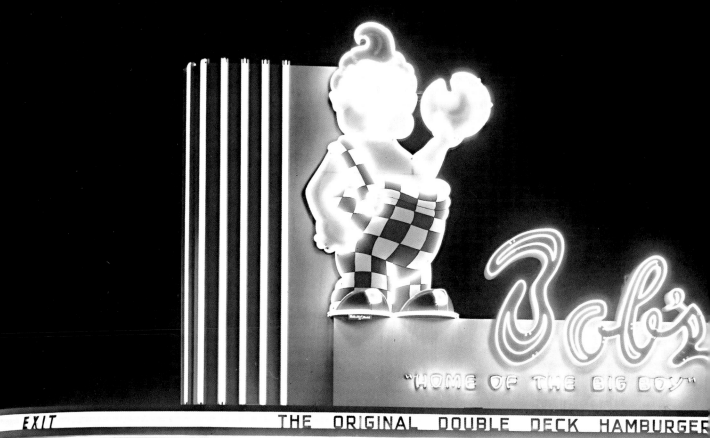

LEFT:
Nighttime neon at Bob's Drive-In. Bob's endured as a spot for young people to see and be seen well into the 1960s and '70s.

ABOVE:
McAllister and architect David Underwood created the earliest Bob's.

Within the illustration:

1801 COLORADO
EAGLE ROCK

Bob's famous DOUBLE DECK HAMBURGER

home of the big boy

PANCAKES   THICKSHAKES

121 E. BROADWAY
GLENDALE

3212 LA CRESCENTA
GLENDALE

HOME OF THE BIG

THE ORIGINAL DOUBLE DECK HAMBURGER

624 S. SAN FERNANDO RD.
BURBANK

ORIGINAL double-deck hamburgers

home of the BIG BOY

910 E. COLORADO
GLENDALE

Bob's HOME OF THE BIG BOY

BIG BOY   *Bob's* HAMBURGER

home of the BIG BOY

5355 VAN NUYS BLVD.
VAN NUYS

CLOCKWISE FROM ABOVE:

Illustration of Bob's in Toluca Lake, Burbank, 1950.

——————

Carhop service at Bob's.

——————

Bob's Drive-In, shortly after completion, 1953.

In the 1990s, the architect joins the fight to save his threatened 1949 Bob's Big Boy building, one of the last of his iconic drive-ins.

highest-grossing coffee shop in the country that doesn't serve alcohol," reports Hansen.

The most visible and dramatic design feature of Bob's is the spectacular neon sign incorporating many of the neon lighting effects learned from the earlier drive-ins. "With neon we could outline the sign. We could give it a third dimension by making the letters deeper and outlining it, or even double or triple outlining it." McAllister told *Sign Builder Illustrated* magazine "we could also use the neon in an indirect manner where we would not actually show the light, but show the outline of the letter without seeing the neon. The tube would be behind throwing its light on the background, not on the letters. All these sorts of things were stunts or devices."

McAllister and his partner William Wagner designed one of his last Bob's Big Boys for Wian in 1951 at 5353 Van Nuys Boulevard. It was a glass box with a stucco overhang with a giant neon sign hung on five square wooden columns, sporting the same dynamic script as the other stores. A two-toned prow marked the entrance, and six black cylinder lamps hung above.

On April 15, 1956, McAllister and Wagner designed a new Bob's Big Boy restaurant opened at 900 East Colorado in Glendale, on the exact site of the first location. The *Los Angeles Times* called it "California's fanciest hamburger joint." One of the most elaborate drive-in restaurants in the entire western United States, it sported a modern color scheme and "pastel shades of pink, green, brown and ivory predominate throughout the interior and exterior with ceramic and mosaic tile being used extensively."

In 1958 the architectural firm of Armet & Davis was chosen to continue expanding the chain to a total

of 750 restaurants at its peak. In 1961 Ontra Cafeteria operator H. Haskell Davenport III attempted a merger with Bob's Big Boy. However, in 1967 McAllister sat in on negotiations with Bob Wian to help the Marriott Corporation acquire the venerable chain.

A decade later there were more than 260 Big Boy's restaurants across the country bearing regional names like Kip's and Azar's and Elias Brothers. "It was a bad situation," Hansen said. "All the stores had been run on the concept of good food and service at reasonable prices, and the corporate guys were bottom-line guys. They were just interested in profits." Another decade passed, and by 1988 Marriott announced they were selling off the Big Boy's chain piecemeal.

Today, Big Boy's restaurants still dot the Midwest, but only a scattered handful remain in Southern California.

GRISINGER'S DRIVE-IN/ GEORGE'S '50s DINER

In 1950 McAllister designed a small drive-in on Long Beach Boulevard at San Antonio Street in Long Beach. Grisinger's is an asymmetrical curving, free-form box of stucco, brick and redwood with a continuous glass storefront of windows and a projecting curved flat roof with a sign tower that also marks the entrance. The abstract geometry is hung around a giant plate-glass window that frames diners and creates visual excitement from the street. In 2004 the restaurant, now named George's '50s Diner, became a Long Beach historic landmark for its design and association with McAllister.

BROWN DERBY DRIVE-IN

In 1940 McAllister was consultant to architect Roland Crawford on the last Brown Derby restaurant; a "car cafe" with drive-in service at the corner of Los Feliz and Hillhurst Avenue in Los Angeles.

TOP:
Grisinger's in Long Beach survives today as George's '50s Diner.

ABOVE:
McAllister worked with architect Roland Crawford on the last Brown Derby located in Los Feliz in 1940.

McDONALD'S

In the early '50s Stanley Clark Meston was a former McAllister employee who developed his own practice in Fontana, a steel mill town about fifty miles east of Los Angeles. Meston did some institutional work and a few car dealerships, but according to McAllister, "he generally starved to death out in that whole area, more or less." In 1952 Meston was approached by Richard and Maurice McDonald to design a new hamburger stand concept they were preparing to franchise. He came up with a canted roof design sheathed in red and white tiles and pierced by two massive parabolic arches fashioned from sheet metal and tied to the building. These "golden arches" were refined by Meston from one of Richard McDonald's designs. "There is a tradition, a continuum in American architecture. From Eliel to Eero Saarinen, from Louis Sullivan to [Frank Lloyd] Wright to John Lautner," says Hess. "Commercial roadside architecture has the same traditions." McAllister noted that Meston "didn't know anything about kitchen designs, so he came to me for the layout of the kitchen, and of course McDonald had some ideas. He and I worked out the plan for the kitchens. The elements of a drive-in, whether it was a Simon's or a McDonnell's or a McDonald's—there were certain things about where you put stuff so you move fast and you get the orders out. A kitchen is laid out around three people. You've got the wheel man, who works at the port where the orders come in and they're hung on a bicycle wheel. He directs the traffic and calls out the orders, and he's got a man on the right and a man on the left. The man on the right is usually the grill man and the man on the left puts more or less everything else together. It's an island. Everything is around that kitchen."

CLIFTON'S CAFETERIA

After WWII, legendary California restaurateur Clifford E. Clinton made plans to expand from his elaborately themed and socially conscious cafeterias in downtown Los Angeles into the new suburb of Lakewood, California. At the time, Clinton noted that "during our twenty-three years in Los Angeles, we have served more than 100,000,000 meals."

In 1953 they contacted McAllister to design the third Clifton's Cafeteria in the 259-acre Lakewood Center, the new town square for the prototypical suburb of Los Angeles. The new restaurant was similar to Ontra Cafeteria and a radical departure from the other Clifton's stores that featured real trees and waterfalls in their fantasy settings.

OPPOSITE AND BELOW:
Clifton's Lakewood location was the third newest, depicting its modern, "California casual" surroundings.

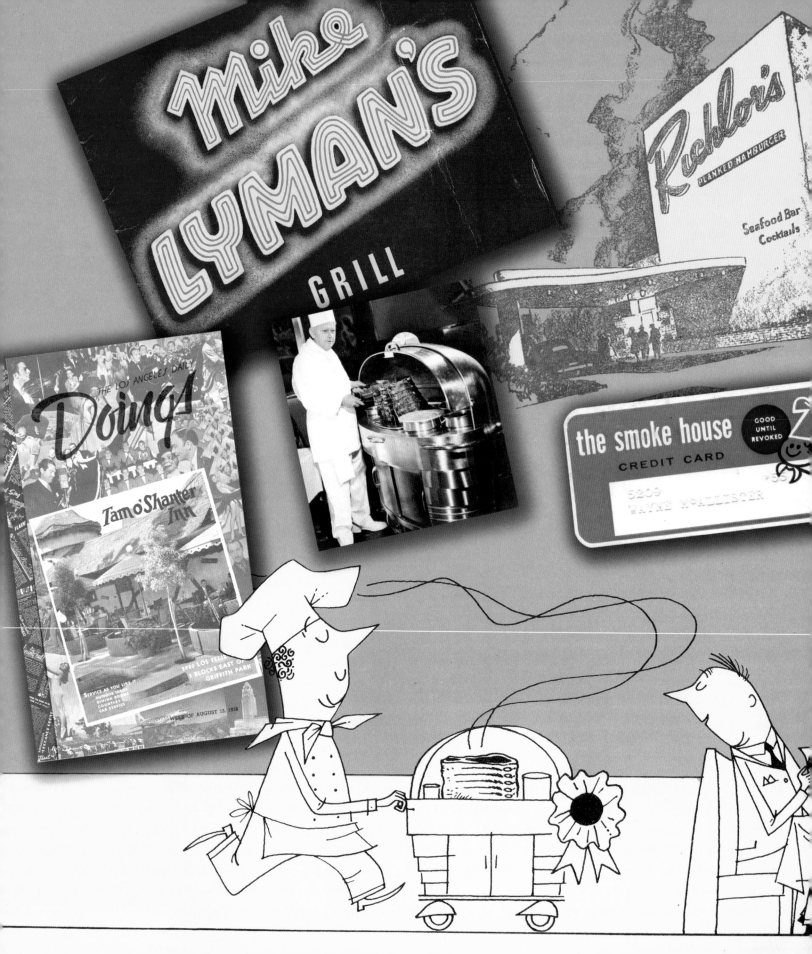

RESTAURANT ROW
LA CIENEGA
Famous Street of Restaurants

THIRD ST.

Eaton's
One of a fine
family

HOUSE OF
MURPHY
Bob Wants
to See You

Tail o' the
Cock
A tale of
fine food

Richlor's
A new
neighbor.

Sarnez
Dancing and
entertainment

Lawry's
THE PRIME RIB
Roast beef from
the silver cart

Jim Otto's
Excelle...
and oth...

MELODY LANE

HOLLYWOOD · WILSHIRE · DOWNTOWN

THE STORY
OF THE
Smoke
House
AND THE
OIL DRUM

Dinner Houses

Dinner Houses

Baron Long's friends in the tightly knit Los Angeles restaurant fraternity were impressed with McAllister's work at the Biltmore Hotel and soon called on him to design new venues for them. Even at the height of the Great Depression, he kept busy designing more and more lavish showplaces for some of the most distinguished names in hospitality. As he had with breweries and racetracks, McAllister would first become an expert in the building type he was to create. He was immersed in the practical matters of creating space. He versed himself in the language of kitchens, for example, and became a sought-after consultant for restaurants seeking to streamline operations. McAllister employee Stanley Meston recalled that "he was one of the most capable men. He was no draftsman, but he had the ability to perceive and then to surround himself with the right people. He knew materials, he knew equipment, he knew how to discuss things with the owner and how to get the end result."

THIS PAGE AND OPPOSITE:
The lavishly appointed interiors of Mike Lyman's were offered for auction before the building was demolished for a high-rise in 1964.

The golden age of the Hollywood nightclub was in the 1930s. By the outbreak of World War II, few new clubs were opening, and the lure of fine dining in a beautiful room began to attract celebrities and the moneyed crowd of what has been called "grown-up Hollywood." By the end of the decade there had been a shift in taste from the photographer-filled hotspots to more intimate venues that offered a quiet refuge.

MIKE LYMAN'S

When restaurateur Mike Lyman died in 1952, Chico Marx and George Burns showed up at his funeral alongside Baron Long, Lyman's and McAllister's old friend. In fact, more than 400 friends from the "glamorous worlds of entertainment and sports, from cafe society and high society" were there. Mike Lyman was big news. The restaurants Mike ran with his brothers Abe Lyman and Bill Simon were revered institutions, lush and lavish showplaces that immediately became centers of Hollywood society and, according to some, "major mafia hangouts."

Lyman came to Los Angeles with his brothers in the 1920s

ABOVE:
Mike Lyman's at Hollywood and Vine. The copper flourishes and neon swirls were visible for blocks in this neighborhood where ABC, CBS and NBC were located.

BELOW:
Melody Lane, formerly the Pig 'n Whistle, began in 1908.

to pursue their vaudeville act. His brother Abe Lyman and his band were the opening act at the Cocoanut Grove at the Ambassador Hotel. The restaurants were just as theatrical: at the Hill Street Lyman's, guests entered under a muscular bronze lion created by the artist Millard Sheets; in Hollywood the sweeping brass curves and flowing triple-neon script so overwhelmed the simple Georgian building that they were visible a block away.

In 1938 *Westways* magazine called Lyman's "a welcome change from the chromium and red leather modernity of some of our better restaurants." McAllister created three of the four Lyman's restaurants, but all featured the rich décor and sumptuous menu of the original. The editor of *Saveur* magazine once called Lyman's menu "an astonishing document" and noted that "over twenty-five varieties of fish and shellfish were offered, including imported Irish salt mackerel and a dish called Fried Barracuda Maitre d'Hotel."

MELODY LANE

Sidney Hoedemaker had great success with his Pig 'n Whistle restaurants. In 1941 he relocated his Hollywood Boulevard store four blocks from its former location near the El Capitan Theatre to the fabled intersection of Hollywood and Vine, and renamed it Melody Lane (see additional information on page 89).

The Hollywood Boulevard location was a co-venture with architect S. Charles Lee. Lee was best known for his fantastic movie theater designs in the 1920s and '30s. Lee and McAllister created a theatrical environment for Melody Lane by remodeling a building originally designed by Richard Neutra into a wraparound signboard with a keyhole cutout for an adjacent cocktail lounge. The name was spelled out like a marquee in larger-than-life neon script above the entrance. The fantastic interiors rendered by Lee featured a swooping, sweeping dining room with almost no corners. A single pendant light fixture, stepped like the Empire State Building, hung from the ceiling. Zigzagging mirrors with planter bases ringed the walls. The counter was an exaggerated sine curve whipping across the length of the room. An adjacent dining area was a series of semiprivate U-shaped banquettes against massive curving pillars draped in fabric and capped with an ornate gold chandelier. The reality was a bit more workaday but still Hollywood enough to hold that corner.

In 1948 Hoedemaker opened his most lavish restaurant to date in Beverly Hills. It had 550 seats and a large cocktail lounge. A collaboration with the artists Albert Stewart and William Manker produced the Puppet Room, which was "uniquely decorated with glazed sculptural figures of famous circus people, dancers and bullfighters in glowing color and lively action," according to one magazine account. The prominent California artist Millard Sheets designed the settings and painted the backgrounds for the themed environment. The puppets were suspended on wires and could assume "action poses."

RICHLOR'S

With the success of McAllister's "Super Twin Drive-In" for Van de Kamp's, the family brought McAllister in to design a new restaurant in Beverly Hills in 1942. Richlor's was the Frank family's second restaurant on La Cienega Boulevard's restaurant row, where it joined Lawry's

Richlor's was a new concept from the owners of Lawry's and Van de Kamp's and was named after the owners' children, Richard and Lorraine. Below, a view of the massive signboard.

Above the "unique seafood bar" at Richlor's were four large black-lit murals depicting frolicking swordfish, playful hermit crabs and the slightly risqué nude King Neptune atop a flying porpoise.

Minks and martinis at Richlor's Seafood Bar.

the Prime Rib, which had opened in a converted brick warehouse structure in 1938. When Lawry's relocated, McAllister redesigned this space as Stear's for Steaks, another Van de Kamp's venture.

Richlor's was a unique new showplace for the Frank family and featured a bottle of their signature seasoned salt on every table. The main entrance was under a free-form porte cochere dappled with down lighting. The supporting cylinder forms a dogleg with the column above, a detail that was picked up at Lawry's and the Sands Hotel a few years later. The exterior elevation was like a battered temple wall, a series of stepped concrete cants reaching up to an open volume bursting with overgrown plant life. Rising some thirty feet above the restaurant was a massive signboard adorned with "Richlor's" in neon script. Inside, Richlor's featured live fish in wall-mounted tanks, and above the "unique seafood bar" were four large black-lit murals whose themes included a frolicking swordfish, some playful hermit crabs, and the slightly risqué nude King Neptune atop a flying porpoise.

In 1960 the family changed the restaurant into The Mediterranea, and in 1984 the building's owners cashed in on the '50s diner craze as the West Coast outlet of Ed Debevic's. In a strange twist of irony, the architectural firm of Armet Davis Newlove, the undisputed kings of the California coffee shop of the 1950s, were employed to renovate Richlor's, product of the 1940s, into a "'50s" restaurant by grafting on an authentic 1930s-style prefabricated diner. The building was demolished in 2004.

TAM O'SHANTER INN

The relationship between McAllister and the Frank family was long lived. He was called in to enlarge and remodel the historic Tam O'Shanter Inn. The Tam was one of Walt Disney's favorite dining spots, located in the Los Feliz district on what had been a quiet country lane opposite the Gladding McBean tile plant. The restaurant opened in 1922 as Montgomery's Country Inn. Richard Frank

TAM O'SHANTER INN
2980 Los Feliz Blvd. • LOS ANGELES

Outdoor dining at the Tam O'Shanter Inn, Walt Disney's favorite restaurant in the Los Feliz section of Los Angeles.

Wayne McAllister and . . .

remembers that "my father called upon the set designer Harry Oliver, who created a fairy-tale-like Norman inn both inside and out." The exterior of the Tam is a series of undulating, lopsided, eaveless cupolas with a gnarled walking stick rising from the center. Stone and stucco with storybook shingle interiors were dark with heavy half timbers supporting medieval iron chandeliers. A massive hearth, big enough to walk inside, dominates one of the dining rooms. Family crests and tartans decorate the walls. Leaded webs of stained glass sit upon brick sills. A mahogany bar with vertical wood facing also sits atop used brick and offers a cozy nook to imbibe or enjoy a roast beef sandwich. Today, the Tam O'Shanter holds the title of oldest restaurant in Los Angeles in its original location with the same family ownership and management.

The expanded dining areas at the Tam O'Shanter Inn were created by McAllister. The restaurant opened as Montgomery's Country Inn in 1922.

The finest dining room created for the Frank family was undoubtedly Lawry's in 1947. McAllister created a grand restaurant that anchored the emerging restaurant row of Beverly Hills. Lawry's had become the finest theme restaurant of the time. McAllister remembered: "It's a little difficult to describe Lawry's because there is nothing else like it architecturally or gastronomically in the United States."

Richard Frank accompanied his father on scouting trips, and remembered "driving around in the car with my father on weekends, searching for the perfect location. His decision to settle for a former restaurant site on La Cienega Boulevard, halfway between Santa Monica and downtown Los Angeles, was another of his fortuitous judgment calls. The area was hardly developed at all. A former swampland, it contained two other restaurants, and many vacant lots were run over with mustard fields. It would grow up to be the world's first and most famous restaurant row."

Lawry's used traditional materials of brick and stone to create a bold modern composition. It was like an English castle for the Eisenhower era. A bay of seven tall windows look out onto a restaurant row guarded by the high undulating rock wall that wraps around the circular room. A wide, flat signboard rises up to double the height of the building and offer a surface to affix the steel letters "L-a-w-r-y-'s." Drivers leave their cars under an adjacent porte cochere finished in matching stone.

In 1964, the *Los Angeles Times* described the scene:

Dinner at Lawry's takes place in a magnificent setting of plush comfort and beautiful appointments. The entrance to the main dining room is guarded by two hand-carved mahogany lions which graced the hall of an English nobleman's ancestral mansion in Northumberland in the garden of the nineteenth century. The main dining room is lined with sculpted booths and checkered with handsome tables and high-back chairs. On the

OPPOSITE, ABOVE:
The dynamic dogleg portico of Lawry's foreshadowed the design of the Las Vegas Sands and created a powerful presence on the nation's first restaurant row in Beverly Hills.

———

OPPOSITE, BELOW:
Lawry's the Prime Rib continues to serve their signature dish from these carving carts, a bulbous creation of stainless steel featured at their original restaurant in 1938.

Lawry's the Prime Rib began in Beverly Hills in 1938. McAllister designed their sleek new home across the street in 1947.

west wall is a huge orange-hued tapestry especially made for Lawry's. The design is based upon the renaissance period in England and includes the emblem of the Order of the Garter. A large illuminated mural on the north wall illustrates a formal English garden of the nineteenth century. The meat is dispensed from a gleaming blimp-like silver cart which is rolled right up to the patron's table.

Lawry's moved to a larger building in 1995 and remains a bastion of fine dining in Los Angeles. Their newest locations are in Jakarta and Las Vegas.

Wayne McAllister and . . .

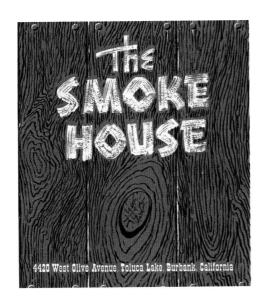

4420 West Olive Avenue, Toluca Lake, Burbank, California

ABOVE:

At the end of WWII, when the General Motors plant in Van Nuys went back to making Pontiacs and tract houses started replacing the San Fernando Valley's bean fields, two Lockheed Aircraft workers named Jack Monroe and Jim Stockton started the Smoke House Restaurant in Burbank.

BELOW:

The Smoke House remains a popular destination opposite the Warner Brothers Studios in Burbank. Members of the film and television community hold wrap parties in its rustic dining rooms.

SMOKE HOUSE RESTAURANT

At the end of WWII, when the GM plant in Van Nuys went back to making Pontiacs, and tract houses started replacing the San Fernando Valley's bean fields, two Lockheed Aircraft workers named Jack Monroe and Jim Stockton started the Smoke House Restaurant in Burbank. In 1946 it was a humble restaurant that seated forty-six people. The Red Coach Inn, a small restaurant opened and owned by actor Danny Kaye, sat empty on a prime lot directly across from Warner Brothers Studios, and in 1955 Wayne McAllister and partner William Wagner were brought in to build a new home for the Smoke House Restaurant. Their rustic Tudor Revival design completely surrounded the existing buildings and was finished with half timbers and river rock. The interior is a maze of lacquered paneling and plush carpeting under a heavy-timbered ceiling. The building is capped with an enormous pink neon "SMOKE HOUSE" sign that reflects in the Los Angeles River below. The following year Jack Parr broadcast *The Tonight Show* from the restaurant as entertainers moved in and made the Smoke House their own. Owner Jim Lucero remembered his first time at the Smoke House as a kid in the '50s: "I loved its feel of excitement. The expanse of the place, the crisp white tablecloths, the red leather, the entertainment and all the people visiting; it was like a party." The cast of *Laugh-In* took over the place for their own riotous parties in the '60s. Actor George Clooney has a plaque on his favorite booth today.

Las Vegas

The Sands
LAS VEGAS, NEVADA

Fremont
LAS VEGAS

WILBUR CLARK'S
$1.00
DESERT INN

EL RANCHO VEGAS

Hotel Fremont
FARO
$5
LAS VEGAS · NEVADA

FREMONT HOTEL
LAS VEGAS

In the heart of the Las Vegas strip, at the southwest corner of Sahara Avenue and Las Vegas Boulevard, sits a huge open parcel of land. Flat and sprawling, this raw chunk of Nevada desert pokes through the carefully manicured illusion and neoclassical trappings of modern Las Vegas. It sits much the way McAllister and Thomas Hull found it in 1938 en route to creating the first luxury resort there and bringing the land of casinos and showrooms to life. McAllister and Hull set about building the very first resort hotel on what would become "the strip." They set out to invent Las Vegas.

EL RANCHO VEGAS HOTEL

In 1938 McAllister was approached by Jack Barkley, a wealthy San Diego socialite who had been impressed with Agua Caliente and with the legalization of gambling in Nevada in 1931. With the influx of workers from the $100 million Boulder Dam project, he speculated that the growing town of 8,000 could become the new vacation destination for Southern California. Mobster Tony Cornero had limited success with a smaller hotel/casino called The Meadows, but it closed after five years. Reformed Los Angeles vice cop Guy McAfee also briefly operated the 91 Club in 1938.

Their report touted McAllister's earlier accomplishment, "The enormous success enjoyed by the Agua Caliente project in Old Mexico is a matter of record and as it is now closed, probably never to reopen as a gambling resort, the erection of a project of this sort, so readily accessible, appears very logical." The preview ads and even the matchbooks called it "The Caliente of Nevada."

This early jumbo matchbook from El Rancho Vegas hails the new resort and Las Vegas as the "Caliente of Nevada."

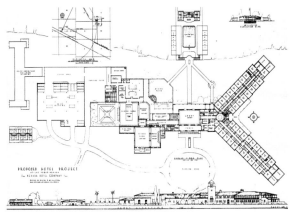

ABOVE:
The earliest rendering and plans for the first hotel on the Las Vegas strip. This drawing was created by McAllister in 1938 to sell a resort just off Highway 91 he was planning with Jack Barkley that would become El Rancho Vegas.

The report predicted that "the combination of a fine hotel with a magnificent gambling casino created an exceptional opportunity for profits. Such new developments are a rare opportunity and when this project is completed it should, without a doubt, be one of the outstanding resorts of its kind on the North American continent." The plan called for a grand galleria running through the center of the California Mission-style design, with shops and restaurants leading to a grand French Room casino. The original plan called for an enclosed garden and outdoor arcades and porches along an arched colonnade.

McAllister and Barkley spent months preparing a business plan for the venture. The Reconstruction Finance Corporation, a Roosevelt-era public works organization that created Mount Rushmore, among other massive works projects during the Depression, supported the plan. With encouragement from Vegas booster James Cashman, hotelier Thomas Hull signed on as the operator, the Reconstruction Finance Corporation offered financial subsidies for 50 percent of the project. The Union Pacific Railroad also agreed to support the hotel aspect but shied away from lending its name to a gambling casino.

For two years the promoters tried unsuccessfully to sell 2,450 shares of stock, priced at $100 per share in the hotel project.

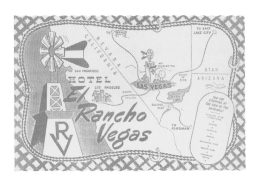

It was predicted that the hotel would create a $240,000 profit that first year. There were no takers. Las Vegans didn't believe the resort would succeed. Even McAllister thought it would close in the summer months like resorts in Palm Springs did. Most extant casinos were separate structures and relied on rowdy working men for customers. When conventional financing collapsed, McAllister approached Los Angeles gamblers, including Nola Hahn, whom he had done work for at the Clover Club, an underground casino on the Sunset strip in Hollywood. Hahn doubted that legal gambling could ever be profitable even after a major crackdown on illegal gambling in California in 1938 by Attorney General Earl Warren.

Even Barkley thought the project was doomed and backed out. McAllister remembered that Barkley was the one with the real vision. He once predicted that Las Vegas would someday be bigger than Miami Beach, a suggestion that caused McAllister to laugh out loud.

However, McAllister and his old friend Hull believed in the project. Hull eventually found a private loan in Texas. To avoid taxes, he located the hotel outside the city limits. He then scaled it back a bit, moved it right up against Highway 91, and modeled it on the series of El Rancho motels that McAllister had previously designed in Fresno and Sacramento, all of which featured rambling cabins, enormous open space and a towering windmill.

El Rancho Vegas opened for business April 3, 1941. Some of the mission-style elements were retained for rows of bungalows that were hidden along winding roads on the sixty-six-acre grounds, but El Rancho was a sprawling, Palm Springs–style luxurious dude ranch complete with working horse stables. The shake roofs were long and low, and the building featured stone fireplaces and board-and-batten walls. A covered walkway ran along the room wings. A collection of Mission-style bungalows was nestled among the western landscaping. These luxury units resembled the bungalows at Agua Caliente; they had their own fireplaces and were occasionally tied together with covered arcades. The enormous swimming pool, placed close to the highway, with stone planters and split-rail fences surrounding the

HOTEL EL RANCHO VEGAS
"Western America's Finest"
LAS VEGAS, NEVADA

STOP AT THE SIGN OF THE WINDMILL

scrubby landscaping, was a terrific sales tool. Rising and spinning above it all was a fifty-foot illuminated windmill, trimmed in pink-and-white neon and marked "El Rancho Vegas," a trademark, a beacon and a logo for the hotel. The windmill was akin to the campanile at Agua Caliente and a precursor to the giant genies, silver slippers and volcanoes that became trademarks for future generations of Vegas hotels.

The casino had an exposed beam ceiling and fixtures modeled on roulette wheels. The twenty-four-hour Chuckwagon Restaurant featured a mural of a stagecoach and horses crossing the dusty Nevada desert. The Round-Up Room was the entertainment hub. An exposed beam ceiling covered in rustic planks soared above such performers as Chico Marx and Pearl Bailey, who were often on stage

Wayne McAllister and . . .

OPPOSITE AND ABOVE: El Rancho was a lavish sixty-six-acre resort featuring large pools, tennis and horseback riding. The hotel kept a boat in Lake Mead, offering fishing and boating for guests.

until dawn. A low rope fence separated the stars from the audience and a small dance floor.

Even in this first resort, all the elements of the postwar Las Vegas strip are present: easy parking, air-conditioning, a lavish casino, a central pool, the room wings, a roadside icon and a massive sign; these became the fundamentals of strip architecture for the next several decades.

In 1942 Joseph Drown, an associate of Conrad Hilton, bought the El Rancho from Hull. McAllister knew Drown from the Town House Hotel remodel in Los Angeles. Hilton and Drown owned hotels but weren't operators. They hired Wilbur Clark, a former bellhop from San Diego, who worked his way up to manager and then operator. When expansions were needed, due to the success of

ABOVE:
Gamblers crowd the craps table at El Rancho Vegas.

RIGHT:
El Rancho neon at dusk beckons visitors along Highway 91.

HOTEL
El RANCHO
VEGAS
FINE FOODS
CASINO
COCKTAIL LOUNGE
100% AIR CONDITION
SWIMMING POO

El Rancho, Clark and Drown hired McAllister to do the work. After more changes in ownership, including L.A. gamblers Farmer Page and Guy McAfee, the El Rancho finally burned to the ground in a mysterious fire in 1960. At 4:20 a.m. on June 17, Betty Grable and Harry James were staging an impromptu comedy routine after hours when a fire broke out in a kitchen adjacent to the Opera House theater. Chorus girls, guests and employees ran from the main building, which was completely destroyed, but guests who occupied cottages were not affected. The signature windmill collapsed into the ruins. The site has been vacant ever since.

EL CORTEZ HOTEL

The same year that El Rancho Vegas opened, the Nevada State Legislature voted to legalize what is now known as off-track betting. Meyer Lansky had a great interest in horse racing results by wire. He and several dozen mobsters fled to Vegas to go legit. Lansky's choice to head up the Nevada gambling operation was flamboyant gangster Benjamin "Bugsy" Siegel. While working on the wire operation, Siegel was impressed with the already-successful El Rancho and the brand-new Last Frontier, which had opened in 1942.

Three years later, Siegel was bookmaking; he teamed up with a few partners to rebuild the El Cortez Hotel on Fremont Street in downtown Las Vegas, gathering a rogue's gallery of future Vegas kingpins, including Gus Greenbaum, Willie Alderman, Davie and Chick Berman, Moe Sedway and Meyer Lansky.

Wayne McAllister was hired to gut the complex and completely rebuild its interiors to function as a casino. World War II was in full swing and building supplies were rationed. However, materials were obtained, and the scope of the big project was hidden behind the brick exterior. The Spanish Colonial Revival hotel received little exterior makeover with the exception of extravagant wraparound neon signage. The group invested $60,000 and sold the hotel six months later for $166,000.

McAllister remodeled the El Cortez on Fremont Street for Bugsy Siegel's operation. He refused Siegel's offer to build the Flamingo four years later.

FLAMINGO HOTEL

Siegel's group took the El Cortez profits and reinvested in a new entity, creating The Nevada Project Corporation. At the same time, Billy Wilkerson, founder of *The Hollywood Reporter* newspaper, came to town looking to finance a casino resort based on the glitz of Café Trocadero, Ciro's and LaRue, his Sunset strip nightclubs. Architect George Vernon Russell, who had created Ciro's, was hired to design the new resort. An underfunded Wilkerson brought in new partners with a group that included Benjamin Siegel, who attempted to discharge Russell and sent his associate Mack Kufferman to offer Wayne McAllister the job of building his new Flamingo Hotel. With wartime rationing still affecting the availability of building materials, McAllister was hesitant about taking the job. Siegel assured him his men would have no problem obtaining the materials, but Wayne became more uncomfortable with the idea of ground-up construction and mountains of illegal lumber stacked out in the open desert and, for the first time in his career, turned down a project. The job reverted to Russell and young contractor Del Webb. The Flamingo set the tone for modern Las Vegas. Some say it was not the hotel but Siegel's murder soon after its completion that brought unprecedented attention to the small gambling town in the desert.

DESERT INN HOTEL

In 1947 El Rancho manager Wilbur Clark had an idea for a casino of his own a few blocks south on the same stretch of Highway 91, and hired Wayne McAllister to design the Desert Inn. McAllister laid out a plan of 229 hotel rooms radiating out in hipped roof wings from a two-story casino, showroom and restaurant. Construction had begun and the frame structure sat for two years while new financing was arranged. Wilbur Clark went to Ohio mobster Moe Dalitz, and with a new syndicate in control, completion of the job fell to Hugh Taylor, a young unlicensed architect. (McAllister said that there were only two licensed architects in Nevada at the time: himself

El Rancho manager Wilbur Clark hired McAllister to design his new 300-room Desert Inn, the fifth resort on the Las Vegas strip.

and an "older gentleman who was pretty much retired.") McAllister's original scheme was left largely intact; Taylor's main contribution was a restaurant and the casino. The Desert Inn followed the lead of the Flamingo—modern but with ranch-house flair. The large neon yucca installed above the Skyroom bar marked the entrance. A row of flagstone columns ran along the lobby arcade, leading to hotel registration and the casino and to acres of lawn with a ring of hotel rooms. This was the most Palm Springs–like resort yet, with a large golf course and a massive circular pool. The Desert Inn was imploded in 2002; the newest section was only four years old. In April 2005 Steve Wynn's "Wynn Las Vegas" opened on the site.

SANDS HOTEL

Five years after Wayne turned down the Flamingo project, Mack Kufferman, a financial manager for Meyer Lansky, again contacted McAllister on the recommendation of Nola Hahn to turn a small French restaurant they had acquired, The La Rue, into a sprawling hotel and casino complex.

The Sands Hotel opened December 15, 1952, and was strictly modern. One of McAllister's most elegant creations, the hotel set the standard for the next generation of hotels in Las Vegas.

Jack Entratter, well known from his Copacabana club in New York, was hired as director of entertainment. On his good name, along with Kufferman and mob figure Joseph "Doc" Stacher, a sham transfer of ownership to Texas gambler Jake Freedman was devised, which diverted attention from Kufferman and Stacher, the true owners of the hotel. Entratter owned two points—the same awarded to McAllister for his design services.

It was unusual for architects to design their own signs; the business belonged almost entirely to the Young Electric Sign Company (YESCO), which designed some of the most spectacular electric signs ever built in Las Vegas, from the three-dimensional Golden Nugget to the atomic Stardust to Vegas Vic, the iconic cowboy sign on Fremont Street. "YESCO's neon creations," noted the *Las*

These oversized doglegs are featured front and center in this stylized rendering of the Sands.

The bold roadside geometry of the Sands.

Poolside at the Sands.

The pool at the Sands was often crowded with sunbathers, but the hotel provided private lawns and a generous amount of sprawling green space. A clay tile screen brings Palm Springs to Las Vegas. Hotel room wings were named after famous racetracks.

OVERLEAF, LEFT:
Sinatra's Rat Pack pose for a group shot during the daytime shooting of *Ocean's 11* (1960). At night they were performing together in the Copa Room.

OVERLEAF, RIGHT:
Pinup photographer Peter Gowland was working with Tallulah Bankhead in the Copa Room when he documented the new casino. This captures the lighting that allows tables at the Sands to be lit and the rest of the room to be dark.

Vegas Review Journal, "became the trademark for Las Vegas, and their glare could be spotted by astronauts orbiting the Earth."

However, McAllister did all of his own sign designs and YESCO fabricated them. "If I let YESCO design a sign," he remembered, "they would be back a couple of years later trying to get you to buy a better one."

The fifty-six-foot egg-crate signboard for the Sands Hotel became the icon of Las Vegas in the '50s. A solid stucco tower rose out of the ground and supported the perforated, asymmetrically cantilevered egg crate. All night long, the sizzling incandescent bulbs started off like a fuse, racing their way up and around the dynamic script lettering—S-A-N-D-S—repeating in red neon and white chasers against the black desert sky.

McAllister's brilliant, sparkling neon bait led to a driveway lined with tall skinny lamps bent from metal, mimicking the dogleg porte cochere. These modern sculptures sat in landscaping and were just about the only thing between the highway and the courtyard pool. The broad shaded entry was a thin plate decorated with dozens of illuminated cans, similar

Greetings from

The Sands

OPPOSITE:
Delicate custom-made modern pipe lighting fixtures line the entrance drive to the Sands Hotel and separate the pool from the driveway and porte cochere.

ABOVE, LEFT:
Furniture manufacturer Barker Brothers created a special advertising section showing the interiors they furnished at the Sands in 1952.

ABOVE, RIGHT:
Wire assemblage art by Tony Duquette adorns the Copa Room at the Sands.

to his design for Lawry's in Beverly Hills. The main entrance was two stories high and faced a wall of Italian marble.

Inside, the old tricks of gambling-hall design came into play. The casino is always placed in the center of the hub so that guests must traverse it on their way to the registration desk, the restaurant and the street. Clocks and windows were banished in the casino, creating a dizzying lack of time orientation and the mistaken reassurance that you had not gambled the night away. The vast, brightly carpeted space was lit by copper chandeliers fashioned to resemble enormous roulette wheels. An elaborate system of catwalks above allowed security to keep an eye on the players.

The main cocktail lounge seated more than 500 guests. Behind the bar, a massive bas-relief mural designed by Albert Stewart, Millard Sheets' protégé, featured broncos, cowboys and the mushroom cloud of the atomic bomb. But the greatest fame of the Sands came from its aggressive entertainment programming. The same acts that performed at Entratter's Copacabana were seen at the Sands' Copa Room. The biggest entertainers clamored for a spot on the bill. Danny Thomas

The Sands had a very active publicity department and constantly furnished pictures of celebrities and bathing beauties to the national press, drawing visitors to the hotel.

opened the showroom on December 15, 1952. Acts ranging from Marlene Dietrich to Lena Horne to Jerry Lewis were booked, and soon Frank Sinatra became a regular presence at the Copa Room; the entire world of the Rat Pack and the swank and swagger of Sinatra, Dean Martin and Sammy Davis Jr. was born on that stage.

Guest rooms were placed in a semicircle around spacious lawns and the half-moon-shaped pool that hosted the Sands' famous "floating craps game." There were four two-story motel wings, each named after thoroughbred racetracks and holding fifty rooms each. The suites, often described as "Bermuda modern," had private lanais divided by egg-crate grilles, references to the hotel's great roadside sign.

The Sands was a respite of "soft colors, soft lights and the cool dimness so blessed in the desert," reported *Harper's* magazine in 1955, "with dewy lawns laid on imported soil and painfully maintained against nature."

In 1967 architect Martin Stern added a cylindrical tower but kept McAllister's garden rooms intact. The hotel continued into its fourth decade until a new hotel was proposed for its site in 1996. On November 26 of that year, the Sands, the most iconic hotel in Las Vegas, was imploded for the elaborately themed Venetian Hotel.

FREMONT HOTEL

The last project McAllister completed in Las Vegas was the Fremont Hotel. After the nine-story Riviera on the strip, it was the first real high-rise tower in a city that became defined by them.

Opened on May 18, 1956, the Fremont loomed over Fremont Street, the historic downtown of Las Vegas. The street terminated one block from the Union Pacific Railroad Depot, the reason this city existed at all. A property auction held here in 1905 sold the first 110 acres of desert scrub in the new city of 800 residents.

The Fremont was conceived by San Francisco theater producer Louis Lurie and was brought to life by McAllister and his partner William Wagner with financing by gangster Eddie Levinson, a partner in the Sands. It brought contemporary luxury and glamour to downtown Las Vegas, boasting top entertainment in its showrooms, a rooftop pool, a spacious casino of more than 30,000 square feet and 200 hotel rooms.

The modern-style concrete hotel is innovative in its use of modular concrete exterior panels. A frame for the thirteen-story hotel was constructed and exterior walls were lifted into place with a crane. They are covered with a pebble aggregate in shades of pink, tan and reddish brown. An enormous integrated blade of thin concrete rises over the roof and down the facade, holding the integrated signage, also designed by McAllister. "While the Riviera was clearly Miami Modern," notes historian Alan Hess, "the Fremont was California Modern." The street-level facade was covered in dramatic yellow, red and black striped tile and it's wide, flat overhangs offered shade and shelter from the desert heat. At night the underside of this canopy came alive in a dizzying explosion of neon, with galloping white and rose spirals ringed by yellow, pink and white waves.

The Carnival Room was the main showroom and was originally finished with enormous chandeliers made from groups of resin-coated plastic cylinders. The décor of the Fremont was probably the closest McAllister came to what we now know as classic mid-century

The modern-style concrete hotel is innovative in its use of modular concrete exterior panels.

OPPOSITE:
Spirals of neon and stripes of tile bring the sidewalk alive at this side entrance to the Fremont Hotel.

ABOVE:
The Carnival Room showroom at the Fremont. Wayne Newton got his start here as a teenage crooner in 1959.

RIGHT:
Fremont Casino, 1956.

CLOCKWISE FROM ABOVE:
Casino floor at the Fremont Hotel; guest rooms; the modern coffee shop at the Fremont was appointed in wire Herman Miller chairs designed by Charles Eames; a travel sticker from the Fremont Hotel, the tallest building in Nevada and the first high-rise hotel in Las Vegas.

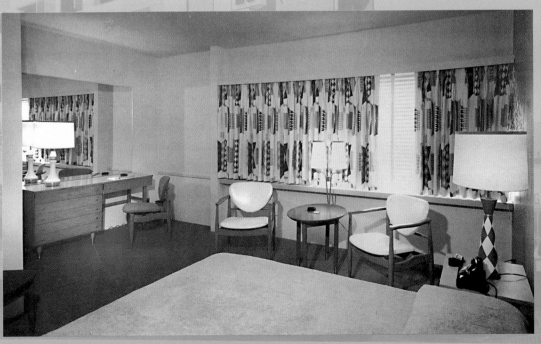

ABOVE:
The neon doglegs of the Horseshoe were the last project on the boards when McAllister left the firm. They are the visual anchor of downtown Las Vegas.

BELOW AND RIGHT:
Meyer Lansky asked McAllister to come to Cuba for the Havana Riviera. He refused the project, which was seized in the Castro revolution.

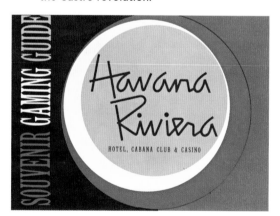

Modern, with the liberal use of Herman Miller furniture designed by Charles Eames.

The intersection of Fremont and Second streets is where all the postcard photographers wanted to be. It defined the look of downtown Las Vegas. "The Horseshoe was on the boards when I left," remembered McAllister. "My partner William Wagner finished it." The glittering prow of the Horseshoe was one of the crowning achievements of Las Vegas neon. Essentially a reworking of the 1905 Apache Hotel, the brick structure was so completely wrapped in its futuristic skin that it disappeared underneath. Dozens of metal fins edged in blue neon ride up and over the roof, an animated light show that culminates in more than a hundred scintillating interlocked H letters coming to life.

HAVANA RIVIERA AND MARRIOTT HOTELS

While working on the Fremont, McAllister was offered the Havana Riviera, a new casino in Cuba being developed by Meyer Lansky, who had been successfully operating the Montmarte in Havana when President Fulgencio Bautista approached him to build new casinos. In 1955 Bautista closed the government-run Nacional and turned

management over to Lansky, who reopened with a bar, restaurant and tax-free casino. Between 1952 and 1955 the number of hotel rooms in Cuba almost doubled.

McAllister cleared his books to make time for the Riviera project. The Fremont was completed and the only thing on the boards in 1956 was the Horseshoe. He was then informed that the entire project from the ground up had to be completed in six months but decided that he couldn't make that pace. Architect Igor Polevitzky eventually designed the hotel. McAllister remembered thinking that he was very lucky—hours after he refused the job, J. Willard Marriott called with a five-year contract and asked him to work for his organization. McAllister thought the timing must be right. The boards were clear, so he left all his project information with his partner, William Wagner, and moved to Washington, D.C.

Fidel Castro made sure the Havana Riviera faced a similar fate as Caliente and was closed in 1960. McAllister's experience in private architectural practice ended where it began: casino gambling closed by a reform government.

McAllister created the first strip hotel, the tallest tower in Nevada and the most iconic resort stage in Las Vegas. His designs set the rhythm and pattern and form of the burgeoning Las Vegas strip and would affect millions.

ABOVE:
The Twin Bridges was Marriott's first hotel. McAllister supervised the construction.

Epilogue

In the twenty-first century Agua Caliente lies in ruins; a government school replaced its core buildings decades ago. The pool and minaret remain as phantom beacons. Not one of McAllister's signature circular drive-in restaurants exists today, their frenetic carhops and throbbing neon forever erased. The Sands Hotel in Las Vegas was imploded to make way for a faux Venice; by the year 2000 gondoliers and canals replaced its bungalows and lawns and pool and "floating craps game."

Sometimes working in historic preservation is like working in a hospice, watching your friends slip away. You hear their stories, get to know where they fit in and how important they were, and then they suddenly disappear. The survivors function as elders, offering a vision of the civilizations that came before you.

To visit an icon like Bob's Big Boy instantly transports you to an almost-lost suburban setting of wide-open spaces, free and abundant parking, ridiculously large signage calling from six blocks away, a rotund mascot perched at the entrance—you can easily remove yourself from a world of parking validation and video monitoring and security guards. Rolling into Bob's on a Friday night with the music and the carhops and the action is immersion in a lost world as fantastic as anything dreamed up by Sir Arthur Conan Doyle.

The success stories are rare. The variable of real estate prices can make "preservation by neglect" the grand savior of historic sites. Land value functioning as the juror of preservation is like picture-frame prices dictating which paintings are saved and which are tossed out.

Depending on a civic solution in Southern California is rare. A tiny handful of the eighty-eight cities in Los Angeles County have preservation plans; even fewer have dedicated staff. Though the City of Los Angeles began its Historic Cultural Monument program in 1963, the first step to becoming proactive about saving buildings, a survey of potentially historic sites has been unfunded for decades.

Sometimes there are exceptions. For example, an enlightened preservation officer for the port city of Long Beach took the unprecedented step of landmarking the only remaining example of a drive-in restaurant in that town. Though the lines of McAllister's 1953 Grisinger's are slightly overwhelmed by its inauthentic *Happy Days* makeover as George's '50s Diner, it remains a beloved gathering spot in the community. Lines for weekend breakfasts and occasional car shows brighten the stretch of historic Highway 15, dulled down by oatmeal strip malls and mirrored office buildings.

LITERATURE

In 1949 Raymond Chandler made McAllister's buildings part of the myth landscape of Phillip Marlowe's Los Angeles in his book *The Little Sister:* "I drove on past the gaudy neons and false fronts behind them, the sleazy hamburger joints that look like palaces under the colors, the circular drive-ins as gay as circuses with the chipper hard-eyed carhops, the brilliant counters, and the sweaty, greasy kitchen that would have poisoned a toad."

MOTION PICTURES

Perhaps most fitting for an architect practicing in Los Angeles is the record of McAllister's architecture in motion pictures:

ABOVE:
The Double H Club was a nightclub for dancing and live music started by Harry Highsmith in 1946. It was located on Route 66 in the Los Angeles community of Eagle Rock. It is shown here shortly before its demolition in 2002.

RIGHT:
The new owners of Richlor's chose to renovate the restaurant, an authentic product of the 1940s, into a "fifties" cafe by grafting on an authentic 1930s-style prefabricated diner! The building was demolished in 2004.

When Jackie Cooper crawled around the exterior of a luxury hotel building, hunting for his boxer pal in *The Champ* (1931), the Oscar-winning film provided a visual record of Agua Caliente. The most lavish depiction of the Mexican resort came in the 1935 Warner Brothers release *In Caliente,* which functioned as a travelogue in the guise of a musical comedy. Pat O'Brien starred as a magazine editor reviewing the dance performance of Dolores del Rio at the hotel. Edward Everett Horton fumbled and bumbled by the pool, and Busby Berkeley staged huge musical numbers, including "The Lady in Red," which was introduced in the film.

When Bob Hope and Bing Crosby were stranded in the Sahara in *Road to Morocco* (1942), the McAllister-designed Herbert's Drive-In, floating in the desert, depicted their mirage of the ultimate dining experience.

Judy Garland played an aspiring actress stuck in the life of washed-up carhop Esther Blodgett in *A Star is Born* (1954). The excised scenes of Judy meeting James Mason in a carhop's majorette uniform were filmed at Roberts Drive-In at Sunset and Cahuenga in Hollywood.

When Lieutenant Colonel Glenn Manning was exposed to an atomic blast in *The Amazing Colossal Man* (1958), he grew to immense size and traded the Nevada Test Site for the Las Vegas strip, where he immediately began tearing apart the Sands Hotel. Several years later Frank Sinatra and friends also tore apart the Sands in a big heist for *Oceans 11* (1960).

STUDIO THEME PARKS

It is also fitting that theme parks re-created work by McAllister. Disney's California Adventure opened next to Disneyland in 2000, featuring a food court with a replica of the Zebra Room. A full-scale circular drive-in clearly modeled on Roberts Drive-In serves as an outdoor dining area. Universal Studios Florida offers a Mel's Drive-In, based on McAllister's Wich Stand design.

The official city of Glendale float in the 2002 Rose Parade depicts McAllister's Bob's Big Boy.

Wayne McAllister

Bibliography

Barell, Barbara. *A Legacy of Light: The History of Young Electric Sign Company.* Camberwell, United Kingdom: Paragon Press, 1995.

Barnard, Charles F. *The Magic Sign: The Electric Art/Architecture of Las Vegas.* Cincinnati: ST Books, 1999.

Basten, Fred E., and Charles Phoenix. *Fabulous Las Vegas in the 50s: Glitz, Glamour & Games.* Santa Monica: Angel City Press, 2003.

Beltran, David Jimenez. *The Agua Caliente Story: Remembering Mexico's Legendary Racetrack.* Lexington, KY: Eclipse Press, 2004.

Best, Katharine, and Katherine Hillyer. *Las Vegas, Playtown U.S.A.* New York: David McKay Company Inc., 1955.

Morgan, Neil Bowen. *Yesterday's San Diego.* Miami: Seemann Publishing, 1976.

Cirigliano, Linda. *Hoot Mon!: The Story of the Tam O'Shanter Inn.* Los Angeles: Lawry's Restaurants, Inc., 1992.

Davis, Margaret L. *The Los Angeles Biltmore: The Host of the Coast.* Los Angeles: Regal Biltmore Hotel, 1998.

Ferrari, Michelle, and Stephen Ives. *Las Vegas: An Unconventional History.* New York: Bulfinch, 2005.

Frank, Richard N. *Lawry's Foods, Inc.: A Blending of Dreams.* New York: Newcomen Society of the United States, 1987.

Gebhard, David, and Harriette Von Breton. *Los Angeles in the Thirties, 1931–1941.* Los Angeles: Hennessey & Ingalls, 1989.

Hansen, Christian. *The Big Boy Story: King of Them All.* Santa Barbara: Haagen Printing, 2002.

Heimann, Jim. *California Crazy and Beyond: Roadside Vernacular Architecture.* San Francisco: Chronicle Books, 2001.

Heimann, Jim. *Car Hops and Curb Service: A History of the American Drive-In Restaurants, 1920–1960.* San Francisco: Chronicle Books, 1996.

Heimann, Jim. *Out with the Stars: Hollywood Nightlife in the Golden Era.* New York: Abbeville Press, 1990.

Henstell, Bruce. *Sunshine and Wealth: Los Angeles in the Twenties and Thirties.* San Francisco: Chronicle Books, 1984.

Hess, Alan, and Andrew Danish. *Palm Springs Weekend: The Architecture and Design of a Midcentury Oasis.* San Francisco: Chronicle Books, 2001.

Hess, Alan. *Googie Redux: Ultramodern Roadside Architecture.* San Francisco: Chronicle Books, 2004.

Hess, Alan. *Googie: Fifties Coffee Shop Architecture.* San Francisco: Chronicle Books, 1986.

Hess, Alan. *Viva Las Vegas: After-Hours Architecture.* San Francisco: Chronicle Books, 1993.

Hillenbrand, Laura. *Seabiscuit: An American Legend.* New York: Random House, 2001.

Jakle, John A., and Keith A. Sculle. *Fast Food: Roadside Restaurants in the Automobile Age.* Baltimore, MD: Johns Hopkins University Press, 2002.

Lacey, Robert. *Little Man: Meyer Lansky and the Gangster Life.* Boston: Little, Brown and Company, 1992.

Land, Barbara, and Myrick Land. *A Short History of Las Vegas.* Reno: University of Nevada Press, 2004.

Langdon, Philip. *Orange Roofs, Golden Arches: The Architecture of American Chain Restaurants.* New York: Knopf, 1986.

Phoenix, Charles. *Southern California in the '50s: Sun, Fun, Fantasy.* Santa Monica: Angel City Press, 2001.

Reid, Ed, and Ovid Demaris. *The Green Felt Jungle.* New York: Pocket Cardinal, 1964.

Roderick, Kevin, and J. Eric Lynxwiler. *Wilshire Boulevard: Grand Concourse of Los Angeles.* Santa Monica: Angel City Press, 2005.

Schwartz, David G. *Suburban Xanadu: The Casino Resort on the Las Vegas Strip and Beyond.* New York: Routledge, 2003.

Sheehan, Jack, ed. *The Players: The Men Who Made Las Vegas.* Reno: University of Nevada Press, 1997.

Sommer, Robin Langley. *Hollywood: The Glamour Years, 1919–1941.* New York: Smithmark Publishers, 1988.

Tennyson, Jeffrey. *Hamburger Heaven: The Illustrated History of the Hamburger.* New York: Warner Books Inc., 1999.

Toback, James. *Bugsy: An Original Screenplay.* Secaucus, NJ: Hollywood Scripts, 1992.

Waldie, D. J. *Holy Land: A Suburban Memoir.* New York: W. W. Norton & Company, 2005.

Wilkerson III, W. R. *The Man Who Invented Las Vegas.* Beverly Hills: Ciro's Books, 2000.

Witzel, Michael Karl. *The American Drive-In Restaurant.* Osceola, WI: MBI, 2002.

Photo Credits

Chris Nichols Collection: cover, back flap (bottom), back cover (left and top right), 1–5, 13 (top), 14 (center), 15 (bottom), 21 (bottom), 22–23, 25, 26 (bottom), 27–28, 29 (top), 32 (all except top left), 33 (all except top center), 34–35, 36 (bottom), 49 (bottom), 51 (top left and right), 52, 54, 57–59, 61–62, 63 (bottom), 64–67, 70, 71 (top left and bottom), 72–77, 78 (top center, far right, bottom center, bottom left), 79, 84 (bottom), 87 (center), 88, 90 (bottom), 92–93, 94 (bottom), 95, 97–98, 101 (bottom), 108–9, 110 (all except center right), 111 (all except top left), 113 (right), 114 (bottom), 115, 118, 120–21, 123, 124 (all except bottom chips), 125 (all except bottom right and chips), 126–28, 129 (bottom), 130–31, 134–38, 139 (top), 140 (20th Century Fox), 143 (left), 144 (left), 149 (top left), 150–52 (bottom center and top right), 153 (left)

Bruce Herman 99

Delmar Watson: 91

Eagle Rock Historical Society: 100

J. Eric Lynxwiler: 81

Jim Heimann Collection: 80, 83, 87 (top and bottom), 94 (top), 101 (top), 103, 104 (top)

Lawry's Restaurants, Inc.: back cover (bottom right), 111 (top left), 116–17, 119, 122

Los Angeles Public Library: 37, 89 (Security Pacific Collection), 90 (top, Security Pacific Collection, 104 (bottom), 105 (Hollywood Citizen News Collection)

Larry Underhill: 7, 152 (right center)

Marc Wanamaker/Bison Archives: back cover (center right), 14 (upper right), 68–69, 71 (right), 78 (bottom right), 82, 84 (top), 85–86, 96, 102, 114 (top)

Marsha Stevenson: 6, 152 (top left and bottom)

McAllister Family Archives: 8, 14 (upper left, center left, left bottom), 15 (top), 16–20, 21 (top), 24, 26 (top), 29 (bottom), 30–31, 32 (top left), 33 (top center), 36 (top), 38–44, 47–48, 49 (top), 50, 51 (bottom left), 53, 55, 60, 78 (top left), 110 (center right), 112, 113 (left), 145–46, 152 (bottom center and right)

Mike Valent: 107

Millennium Biltmore Hotel Archives: 20, 63 (top)

Pasadena Tournament of Roses Archives: 154

Peter Gowland: 13 (right), 141

Roger W. Vargo/Los Angeles Daily News: 106

Steve Fischer: 124 (chips), 125 (chips)

University of Nevada, Las Vegas: 10–13 (right), 125 (bottom right), 149 (all except top left), 129 (top), 132–33, 139 (bottom), 142–43 (right), 144 (right), 147–48, 152 (center left)

Volker Corell: back flap (top)

Index